PEOPLE'S BIBLE

EZRA
NEHEMIAH
ESTHER

JOHN F. BRUG

PBC

CONCORDIA PUBLISHING HOUSE · SAINT LOUIS

Revised edition first printed in 2005.
Copyright © 1994 Concordia Publishing House
3558 S. Jefferson Ave., St. Louis, MO 63118-3968
1-800-325-3040 • www.cph.org

Commentary and pictures are reprinted from EZRA/NEHEMIAH/ ESTHER (The People's Bible Series), copyright © 1985 by Northwestern Publishing House. Used by permission.

Interior illustrations by Glenn Myers.
The maps and chart by Northwestern Pubishing House staff in consultation with Dr. Brug.

Manufactured in the United States of America

ISBN 0-7586-0425-4

1 2 3 4 5 6 7 8 9 10   14 13 12 11 10 09 08 07 06 05

CONTENTS

ILLUSTRATIONS

MAPS

EDITOR'S PREFACE

The *People's Bible Commentary* is just what the name implies—a Bible and commentary for the people. It includes the complete text of the Holy Scriptures in the popular New International Version. The commentary following the Scripture sections contains personal applications as well as historical background and explanations of the text.

The authors of the *People's Bible Commentary* are men of scholarship and practical insight gained from years of experience in the teaching and preaching ministries. They have tried to avoid the technical jargon which limits so many commentary series to professional Bible scholars.

The most important feature of these books is that they are Christ-centered. Speaking of the Old Testament Scriptures, Jesus himself declared, "These are the Scriptures that testify about me" (John 5:39). Each volume of the *People's Bible Commentary* directs our attention to Jesus Christ. He is the center of the entire Bible. He is our only Savior.

We dedicate these volumes to the glory of God and to the good of his people.

The Publishers

GENERAL INTRODUCTION TO EZRA, NEHEMIAH, ESTHER

Importance

Ezra, Nehemiah, and Esther have not been as popular or widely studied as some of the other historical books of the Old Testament. But they are very important for an understanding of God's plan of salvation. In these books we see how the God of heaven and earth controlled the history of the great empires of the ancient world to serve his purposes.

In this part of Israel's history, the Lord did not rule through mighty miracles as he did when he broke the power of Egypt through the ten plagues. He did not rule through supernatural intervention, as he did when he delivered Daniel from the lions' den or Daniel's three friends from the fiery furnace. In these three books we see how the Lord ruled over the kings of the earth with quiet power, which the kings hardly noticed. Without realizing it, four kings of Persia—the greatest empire in the world at that time—became the servants of God's servants.

Because of God's ruling, a remnant of God's people returned from captivity in Babylon to the land of Israel. Behind God's working lay his promises of the Savior. The land of Judah was repopulated so that the Messiah could be born in Bethlehem—just as the prophet Micah had foretold. In Jerusalem, worship and prayer at the temple were restored, and the study of God's Word was revived—so that when the Messiah came, he would be welcomed by a remnant of believers like Zechariah, Elizabeth, Simeon, Anna, Joseph, and Mary.

1

We Christians do not read the books of Ezra, Nehemiah, and Esther merely to learn some interesting ancient history. As we study these books, we marvel at God's grace to an undeserving people and rejoice in the Lord's faithfulness to his promises. God's grace and faithfulness to Israel prepared the entire world for the coming of Christ.

Thanks to God's actions in the past, we can now receive grace through Christ. And as we see how God fulfilled his promises to Israel, we are assured that he will keep his promises to us. Through the example of believers like Ezra and Nehemiah, we learn to trust God as they did. Like them, we also live in a world that opposes God's people and plans. In the books of Ezra, Nehemiah, and Esther, we will see again the truthfulness of the promise "In all things God works for the good of those who love him" (Romans 8:28).

Background

More than any other religion, Christianity is a religion of history. Other religions are made up primarily of legends, myths, and laws that don't depend on a real historical setting. But our Christian faith rests on the acts of God that he carried out in history. To understand God's plan of salvation, we must understand how he used real people who lived at definite times and in real places to carry out his plans. To understand the stories of the Old Testament well, we need to know something about the historical circumstances surrounding them.

None of the Old Testament stories or books are meant to stand by themselves as independent short stories. They are really chapters of one long story—a story that stretches from Eden to Bethlehem. It is the grand story of how God fulfilled his promise and brought his Son into the world. To understand how the "chapters" about Ezra, Nehemiah, and Esther fit into the whole story of the fulfillment of God's plan, we need to review the events that came before and after the time of Ezra, Nehemiah, and Esther. A brief review of the history preceding these books will help us understand how the Israelites had gotten into the sad situation in which they found themselves at the beginning of the book of Ezra.

In the years immediately before the events of Ezra, Nehemiah, and Esther, the tiny nation of Israel had been overwhelmed by the great superpowers of Assyria, Babylon, and Persia. We must go back over three hundred years in the history of Israel to understand how and why this had happened. After the death of King Solomon in 931 B.C., the nation of Israel split into two rival kingdoms. The southern kingdom, called Judah, continued to follow the descendants of David. The worship of the true God continued in Jerusalem, but the people often worshipped idols as well. The northern kingdom, called Israel, was ruled by a number of different dynasties, all of whom supported idolatrous worship. God sent many prophets to warn both kingdoms against their idolatry, but the warnings were ignored. These idolatrous practices continued for about two centuries. Finally, God's patience came to an end. He used heathen empires to bring judgment on his rebellious people.

In 722 B.C. Assyria attacked Israel and carried the ten tribes of Israel into captivity in Assyria. At this time the southern kingdom of Judah also suffered the devastation of war, but God spared it from complete destruction. The escape was only temporary. In 605 B.C. Nebuchadnezzar, king of Babylon, attacked Judah and began a series of deportations in which Daniel, Ezekiel, and many other Jews were taken off to captivity in the land of Babylon. When Zedekiah, king of Judah, rebelled against Babylonian rule, Nebuchadnezzar destroyed the temple and the city of Jerusalem in 586 B.C. More Jews were carried into captivity at this time.

It looked as though Israel's history as a nation had come to an end. But the prophets Isaiah and Jeremiah had prophesied that Israel would return from captivity. The prophets

Ezekiel and Daniel kept this hope alive among the people during the 70 years of captivity in Babylon.

The relationship of Ezra, Nehemiah, and Esther

The history recorded in the book of Ezra begins in 539 B.C. as the 70 years of captivity are coming to a close. Cyrus the Persian had just captured Babylon. Cyrus then permitted Zerubbabel, the prince of Judah, to lead a group of the Jewish exiles back to Judah and authorized them to rebuild the temple in Jerusalem. The first six chapters of Ezra describe these events.

The story of Esther tells how a Jewish woman became queen of Persia and saved the people of Israel from the destructive plot of Haman. These events occurred in about 480 B.C., about 50 years after the return led by Zerubbabel.

Esther's deliverance of the Jews preserved the small group of Jews struggling to survive in Jerusalem. It also made it possible for a larger group of exiles to return to Judah in about 450 B.C. under the leadership of Ezra and Nehemiah.

Ezra and Nehemiah also carried out religious and political reforms necessary for the well-being of God's people. Religious reform was the main work of Ezra the priest. Although Nehemiah was mainly involved in rebuilding the walls of Jerusalem, he too was interested in the spiritual well-being of Israel. The events of this second return are described in the last half of the book of Ezra and in the book of Nehemiah.

The relationship of the three books is illustrated in the chart on the following page. It may be helpful to consult this chart from time to time during your study of these three books in order to see the connection between the events described in these three books and the various kings and prophets who played important roles in the history of God's people.

TIME CHART OF EZRA-NEHEMIAH-ESTHER

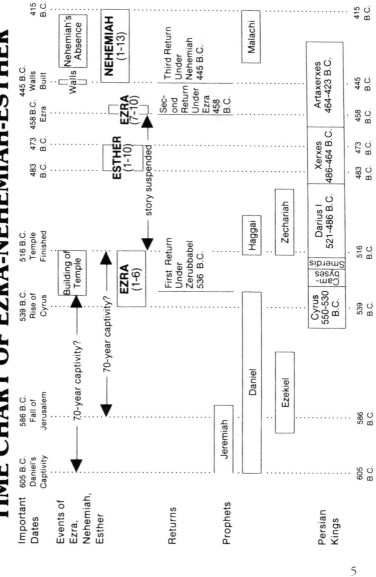

INTRODUCTION TO EZRA

Background

The book of Ezra consists of two distinct parts that report two different phases of the restoration of the nation of Judah. The first is the return from the Babylonian captivity under the leadership of Zerubbabel, prince of Judah, in about 538 B.C. Although this group resettled Judah, they failed to complete the restoration of the temple until they were encouraged by the prophets Haggai and Zechariah almost 20 years after they had first returned. The first six chapters of Ezra describe this time period.

There is a gap of over 50 years between Ezra chapter 6 and chapter 7. During this period Esther saved the Jews from destruction. Chapters 7 through 10 of Ezra take up the events in Jerusalem about 20 years after the time of Esther. These chapters tell how Ezra led a second return from Babylon and carried out a reformation of the religious life of Israel. The greatest problem facing Ezra was Israel's relapse into the practice of intermarrying with heathen neighbors.

Ezra was an excellent teacher of God's Word. He devoted his life to increasing the people's knowledge and understanding of God's law. According to Jewish tradition, Ezra played an important role in the gathering of the individual books of God's Word into the collection that we today call the Old Testament. Ezra probably wrote the book that bears his name; much of the second half of the book is written in the first person. Because Ezra was not a participant in the events described in the first half of the book, he may very well have used written and oral sources available to him to write that part of the book. The inspired writers of Scripture often used written documents or interviews in composing their books, and the Holy Spirit guided their use of such sources to preserve them from error. Since the book of Ezra begins where 2 Chronicles ends and seems to be a sequel to Chronicles, it is possible that Ezra also wrote the Chronicles as a review of the history of Israel up to his own time.

There is some uncertainty about the exact relationship between the books of Ezra and Nehemiah as well as about the relationship between the work of these two men. This problem will be discussed in the commentary on the book of Nehemiah. Since the book of Ezra does not specifically name Ezra as its author, some commentators believe that an unknown author wrote Chronicles, Ezra, and Nehemiah, using the memoirs of Ezra and Nehemiah as two of his main sources. But it's more likely that Ezra himself was the author of Chronicles and Ezra.

The main theme of the book of Ezra is the contrast between God's grace and human sinfulness. God had graciously restored Israel to the land of promise. And how did the people of Israel show their thankfulness? They neglected the rebuilding of his temple. They became discouraged by the opposition from their enemies. They slid back into the same old sin of intermarriage with their heathen neighbors, which had plagued their ancestors. Nevertheless, God sent the prophets Haggai and Zechariah and the priest Ezra to get them back on course so that the nation would be prepared for the coming of the long-awaited Messiah.

The study of the book of Ezra will be a great blessing to us. This book provides much hope and encouragement for the people of God today. It encourages us to work faithfully in the great task of building the church of God. Ezra built up God's people by bringing more people to share in the task of rebuilding Jerusalem and by instructing the inhabitants of Jerusalem with God's Word. Today we build up God's people through evangelism, mission work, and every form of Christian preaching and teaching, which strengthens our fellow Christians in their loyalty to God and his Word. The book of Ezra helps us overcome discouragement as we carry out this work for God because it shows us that no opposition can stop us when we are following the Lord's commission. We are warned not to become trapped in the snares of the enemy as many in Israel were. We are urged to repent as the people of Israel did and to put away the sins that weigh us down and hinder our work for God.

May the study of this book increase our dedication to building the church of God through the worldwide preaching of the gospel! And may it inspire us to be faithful to our calling, just as Ezra and other heroes of the faith have been in the past!

Outline

    I. The first return (1:1–6:22)
      A. Cyrus authorizes the exiles to return (1:1-11)
      B. The list of the exiles who returned (2:1-70)
      C. Rebuilding the altar and the temple (3:1-13)
      D. Opposition to the rebuilding (4:1-24)
      E. The temple successfully rebuilt (5:1–6:22)

    II. The second return (7:1–10:44)
      A. The return of Ezra (7:1–8:36)
      B. The problem of intermarriage (9:1–10:44)

PART ONE

The First Return
(1:1–6:22)

In Ezra chapters 1 to 6 we will see how the first group of Israelite exiles returned from captivity under the leadership of Zerubbabel. With the encouragement of the prophets Haggai and Zechariah, the people rebuilt the temple despite the opposition of their enemies.

Cyrus authorizes the exiles to return

Cyrus' decree

1 **In the first year of Cyrus king of Persia, in order to fulfill the word of the LORD spoken by Jeremiah, the LORD moved the heart of Cyrus king of Persia to make a proclamation throughout his realm and to put it in writing:**

²"This is what Cyrus the king of Persia says:

"'The LORD, the God of heaven, has given me all the kingdoms of the earth and he has appointed me to build a temple for him at Jerusalem in Judah. ³Anyone of his people among you—may his God be with him, and let him go up to Jerusalem in Judah and build the temple of the LORD, the God of Israel, the God who is in Jerusalem. ⁴And the people of any place where survivors may now be living are to provide him with silver and gold, with goods and livestock, and with freewill offerings for the temple of God in Jerusalem.'"

Cyrus, the great king who founded the Persian Empire, conquered Babylon in 539 B.C. The fall of Babylon (described in Daniel chapter 5) took place approximately 70 years after

Daniel and the first exiles had been led into captivity by Nebuchadnezzar of Babylon.

Jeremiah the prophet had foretold that the Babylonian captivity would last 70 years (Jeremiah 25:11,12; 29:10). This 70 years may refer to the time from the first deportation from Judah in 605 B.C. until those who returned under Zerubbabel were reestablished in the Promised Land in 536 B.C., or it may refer to the time from the destruction of the temple in 586 B.C. to its restoration in 516 B.C. Almost two hundred years before Cyrus commanded the restoration of Israel, Isaiah had prophesied that Cyrus would be the deliverer of Israel (Isaiah 44:28; 45:1). Ezra thus begins his book by emphasizing the Lord's faithfulness to the promise he had given through his prophets.

Ezra shows the historical reality of the fulfillment of this promise by quoting from the actual decree of Cyrus. He very likely had access to such documents because of his connection with the Persian court. The religious language of this decree does not mean that Cyrus was a true believer in the God of Israel. Other historical documents—such as the "Cyrus Cylinder," which reports Cyrus's restoration of the temples of Babylon—show that Cyrus restored many temples. The fact that the language of Cyrus's decree sounds very "biblical" may very well be due to the influence of Daniel or other Jews in the court of Cyrus. They may even have composed the decree for him and pointed out the prophecies of Isaiah that name him as the restorer of Judah.

The historical authenticity of this decree is supported by its similarity to other Persian decrees that have survived. These other decrees also use language honoring the religion of the people to whom they were addressed. Cyrus' role in the release of Israel was not due to his conversion to faith in the God of Israel. Cyrus was like a rich person today who may make donations to all religions as part of his general charity. Cyrus felt all religions were useful. In supporting all of them, Cyrus hoped to gain favor with the many different nationalities and religions in his empire. If he had been made aware of the prophecies of Isaiah, he may have been flattered that he was mentioned in the religious writings of a distant nation.

Although Cyrus had his own motives for releasing Israel, his action is nevertheless an example of how the Lord of nations can use even a heathen king to serve his purposes. Centuries later, at the time of Jesus' birth, God would use Caesar Augustus and Herod to help carry out his divine plans.

Many of the people respond

⁵Then the family heads of Judah and Benjamin, and the priests and Levites—everyone whose heart God had moved—prepared to go up and build the house of the LORD in Jerusalem. ⁶All their neighbors assisted them with articles of silver and gold, with goods and livestock, and with valuable gifts, in addition to all the freewill offerings. ⁷Moreover, King Cyrus brought out the articles belonging to the temple of the LORD, which Nebuchadnezzar had carried away from Jerusalem and had placed in the temple of his god. ⁸Cyrus king of Persia had them brought by Mithredath the treasurer, who counted them out to Sheshbazzar, the prince of Judah.

⁹This was the inventory:

gold dishes	30
silver dishes	1,000
silver pans	29
¹⁰gold bowls	30
matching silver bowls	410
other articles	1,000

¹¹In all, there were 5,400 articles of gold and of silver. Sheshbazzar brought all these along when the exiles came up from Babylon to Jerusalem.

The preservation of the sacred temple vessels, which allowed for them to be restored to the temple, was a special blessing of God's grace. It is clear that Cyrus gave the returnees a very rich collection of precious metal articles for use in the temple, since the total of 5,400 articles greatly exceeds the number of articles enumerated in the list. The meaning of some items in the list is uncertain. The Hebrew term translated as "silver pans" may refer to knives or some other objects used in the temple sacrifices.

The identity of Sheshbazzar, prince of Judah, is a historical problem. In Ezra chapter 2 the leader of the returnees is Zerubbabel, not Sheshbazzar. The most likely explanation is that Sheshbazzar and Zerubbabel were two different names for the same person. This was a common occurrence in ancient times. Daniel, Shadrach, Meshach, Abednego, and Esther all had two names. Both Sheshbazzar and Zerubbabel had the title Governor of Judah, and both are credited with laying the foundation of the temple (Ezra 5:14-16; Haggai 1:1). These coincidences support the theory that they were actually the same person. Since the governor is called Sheshbazzar in a letter to the Persian king, Sheshbazzar was probably the name by which he was known to the Persians, while Zerubbabel was the name that he used among the Jews. Other interpreters have suggested that Sheshbazzar was an older relative of Zerubbabel who quickly faded from the picture. This is based partly on the fact that Zerubbabel had an uncle named Shenazzer, whom some have identified with Sheshbazzar (1 Chronicles 3:17,18). Since the book of Ezra does not specifically identify Sheshbazzar and Zerubbabel, this second interpretation is possible, but the first explanation seems more probable.

One of the most important thoughts of this section is expressed by the phrase, "Everyone whose heart God had moved . . . prepared to go up." Willing hearts are necessary if God's work is to prosper. Willing hearts are the gift of the Holy Spirit, who works in God's people and makes them eager to work for the Lord. It seems that many of the exiles were unwilling to leave the prosperity of Babylon for the difficulties of the journey to Zion and the hard labor of rebuilding God's house. Some who were not moved to make the journey themselves instead gave their support to those who were undertaking the mission on behalf of the whole people of Israel.

The example of those "whose heart God had moved" encourages us to sacrifice willingly for the sake of the gospel. We should also gladly support that work of God's kingdom which we cannot undertake in person. This chapter challenges each one of us to ask, Am I willing to face hardships and make sacrifices to help the people of God build his church here on earth? May the Holy Spirit give us willing hearts so that we are ready to answer with a resounding yes!

The list of the exiles who returned

The lay leaders

2 Now these are the people of the province who came up from the captivity of the exiles, whom Nebuchadnezzar king of Babylon had taken captive to Babylon (they returned to Jerusalem and Judah, each to his own town, ²in company with Zerubbabel, Jeshua, Nehemiah, Seraiah, Reelaiah, Mordecai, Bilshan, Mispar, Bigvai, Rehum and Baanah):
The list of the men of the people of Israel:

³the descendants of Parosh	2,172
⁴of Shephatiah	372
⁵of Arah	775
⁶of Pahath-Moab (through the line of Jeshua and Joab)	2,812
⁷of Elam	1,254
⁸of Zattu	945
⁹of Zaccai	760

¹⁰of Bani	642
¹¹of Bebai	623
¹²of Azgad	1,222
¹³of Adonikam	666
¹⁴of Bigvai	2,056
¹⁵of Adin	454
¹⁶of Ater (through Hezekiah)	98
¹⁷of Bezai	323
¹⁸of Jorah	112
¹⁹of Hashum	223
²⁰of Gibbar	95
²¹the men of Bethlehem	123
²²of Netophah	56
²³of Anathoth	128
²⁴of Azmaveth	42
²⁵of Kiriath Jearim, Kephirah and Beeroth	743
²⁶of Ramah and Geba	621
²⁷of Micmash	122
²⁸of Bethel and Ai	223
²⁹of Nebo	52
³⁰of Magbish	156
³¹ of the other Elam	1,254
³²of Harim	320
³³of Lod, Hadid and Ono	725
³⁴of Jericho	345
³⁵of Senaah	3,630

It's easy to pass over long lists of names like this, because we have a hard time understanding them or seeing any significance in them. This list of names was undoubtedly more meaningful to Ezra and his contemporaries than it is to us. But like all Scripture, this list is written for our learning too.

This list is a testimony to God's goodness in preserving the identity of his chosen people in spite of a 70-year captivity in a far-off land. With Zerubbabel and Jeshua as their leaders, the people remained under the leadership of

David's royal line and of the high priests descended from Aaron. Zerubbabel was the grandson of Jehoiachin, one of the last kings of Judah, who had been carried into captivity in Babylon. The text of Ezra chapter 2 lists only 11 leaders of the return, but the parallel passage in Nehemiah chapter 7 lists 12 leaders, probably to indicate the completeness of this group as a true restoration of Israel.

There are some difficulties in the list itself. From Parosh through Gibbar, the returnees seem to be classified by the names of their ancestors. From Bethlehem through Senaah, they appear to be classified by their hometowns. Some of the terms, such as Elam and Immer, seem to be the names both of towns and individuals. Most of these towns are in the vicinity of Jerusalem (see the map entitled "Judah after the return," page 200). There are also differences between the lists of Ezra and Nehemiah in some of the names and some of the numbers. We will discuss this problem in the commentary on Nehemiah chapter 7.

The temple workers

³⁶The priests:

the descendants of Jedaiah (through the family of Jeshua)	**973**
³⁷of Immer	**1,052**
³⁸of Pashhur	**1,247**
³⁹of Harim	**1,017**

⁴⁰The Levites:

the descendants of Jeshua and Kadmiel (through the line of Hodaviah)	**74**

⁴¹The singers:

the descendants of Asaph	**128**

⁴²The gatekeepers of the temple:

the descendants of Shallum, Ater, Talmon, Akkub, Hatita and Shobai	**139**

⁴³The temple servants:

the descendants of
Ziha, Hasupha, Tabbaoth,
⁴⁴Keros, Siaha, Padon,
⁴⁵Lebanah, Hagabah, Akkub,
⁴⁶Hagab, Shalmai, Hanan,
⁴⁷Giddel, Gahar, Reaiah,
⁴⁸Rezin, Nekoda, Gazzam,
⁴⁹Uzza, Paseah, Besai,
⁵⁰Asnah, Meunim, Nephussim,
⁵¹Bakbuk, Hakupha, Harhur,
⁵²Bazluth, Mehida, Harsha,
⁵³Barkos, Sisera, Temah,
⁵⁴Neziah and Hatipha

⁵⁵The descendants of the servants of Solomon:

the descendants of
Sotai, Hassophereth, Peruda,
⁵⁶Jaala, Darkon, Giddel,
⁵⁷Shephatiah, Hattil,
Pokereth-Hazzebaim and Ami

⁵⁸The temple servants and the descendants of the servants
of Solomon   392

⁵⁹The following came up from the towns of Tel Melah, Tel
Harsha, Kerub, Addon and Immer, but they could not show that
their families were descended from Israel:

⁶⁰The descendants of Delaiah, of Tobiah and of Nekoda   652

⁶¹And from among the priests:

The descendants of Hobaiah, Hakkoz and Barzillai (a man
who had married a daughter of Barzillai the Gileadite
and was called by that name).

⁶²These searched for their family records, but they could not
find them and so were excluded from the priesthood as unclean.
⁶³The governor ordered them not to eat any of the most sacred food
until there was a priest ministering with the Urim and Thummim.

After the laypeople have been listed, various classes of
temple workers are listed. According to 1 Chronicles chapter 24, David had divided the priesthood into 24 orders. It
appears that representatives of only four priestly orders

returned with Zerubbabel. The Levites were also rather poorly represented. This poor representation and the special call for temple workers that Ezra issues in 8:15-17 suggest that the priests and Levites were especially reluctant to leave their new homes in Babylon.

The temple servants and servants of Solomon were probably the descendants of heathen Canaanites who had been forced to perform the menial tasks needed for the temple service (Joshua 9:27; 2 Chronicles 2:17,18). If so, their preservation as part of God's people and their willingness to return are a special demonstration of God's grace.

Those who could not prove their ancestry were not allowed to function in the priesthood since only descendants of Aaron were eligible to serve (Exodus 29:44). If people of doubtful ancestry had been allowed to serve, the validity of the sacrifices offered by these priests would have been in doubt. The people's confidence in their worship and in the forgiveness of their sins could have been undermined. The people of doubtful ancestry would be admitted to the privileges of the priesthood only if their ancestry was confirmed by a direct message from God. One way that such messages had been received before the exile was through the Urim and Thummim. These were objects connected in some way with the breastplate of the high priest (Exodus 28:30). We do not know exactly what they were or how they worked. The book of Ezra does not tell us whether their use was ever restored after the captivity or this remained merely a hypothetical possibility. Perhaps they had been destroyed in the fall of Jerusalem. We do not know whether any priests were restored to service by means of the Urim and Thummim.

The returnees arrive in Jerusalem

[64]The whole company numbered 42,360, [65]besides their 7,337 menservants and maidservants; and they also had 200

men and women singers. **⁶⁶They had 736 horses, 245 mules,
⁶⁷435 camels and 6,720 donkeys.**

⁶⁸When they arrived at the house of the LORD **in Jerusalem,
some of the heads of the families gave freewill offerings toward the
rebuilding of the house of God on its site. ⁶⁹According to their ability they gave to the treasury for this work 61,000 drachmas of gold,
5,000 minas of silver and 100 priestly garments.**

**⁷⁰The priests, the Levites, the singers, the gatekeepers and the
temple servants settled in their own towns, along with some of the
other people, and the rest of the Israelites settled in their towns.**

The return of about 50,000 people was undoubtedly
much smaller than the total killed or deported by the
Assyrians and Babylonians. Yet it was a good start toward
rebuilding Judah. The previous list of the returnees is not a
complete accounting of all the returnees since it totals con-
siderably less than 42,000. The comparatively small number
of animals suggests that the Israelites were no longer a pre-
dominantly agricultural people during the captivity. It may
also indicate the relatively low economic status of those
who were willing to return.

The closing verses of the chapter again emphasize the
grace of God. By his grace the people were established in
the towns of their homeland. In grateful response they gave
freewill offerings according to their ability. Rather than feeling that they were doing God a favor by leaving their Babylonian homes, the people recognized what a privilege it
was to participate in the rebuilding of God's temple. Grateful hearts produced generous offerings. Our offerings as
New Testament believers are to be based on the same principle (1 Corinthians 16:2; 2 Corinthians 8:8-15). The words
of Saint Paul apply to believers of all times: "Each man
should give what he has decided in his heart to give, not
reluctantly or under compulsion, for God loves a cheerful
giver" (2 Corinthians 9:7).

Rebuilding the altar and the temple

Rebuilding the altar

3 **When the seventh month came and the Israelites had settled in their towns, the people assembled as one man in Jerusalem.
²Then Jeshua son of Jozadak and his fellow priests and Zerubbabel son of Shealtiel and his associates began to build the altar of the God of Israel to sacrifice burnt offerings on it, in accordance with what is written in the Law of Moses the man of God. ³Despite their fear of the peoples around them, they built the altar on its foundation and sacrificed burnt offerings on it to the LORD, both the morning and evening sacrifices. ⁴Then in accordance with what is written, they celebrated the Feast of the Tabernacles with the required number of burnt offerings prescribed for each day. ⁵After that, they presented the regular burnt offerings, the New Moon sacrifices and the sacrifices for all the appointed sacred feasts of the LORD, as well as those brought as freewill offerings to the LORD. ⁶On the first day of the seventh month they began to offer burnt offerings to the LORD, though the foundation of the LORD's temple had not yet been laid.**

The returnees put first things first when they made the temple sacrifices one of their priorities. The seventh month of the religious calendar was an ideal time to do this, for it was the greatest festival month of the Jewish calendar. The first day of the seventh month, the Feast of Trumpets, was New Year's Day in the civil calendar. It occurs at the time of the autumn solstice and is still celebrated today as the Jewish New Year, *Rosh Hashanah*. The tenth day of the month was the great Day of Atonement, the day when special sacrifices were made for the sins of the people and the one day of the year when the high priest entered the Most Holy Place. The omission of this most important day from this account is probably due to the fact that the Most Holy Place (also known as the Holy of Holies) had not yet been rebuilt. On the 15th day of the month, the weeklong Feast of Tabernacles began. During this time the people lived in booths to commemorate their 40 years in the wilderness. This holiday also served as a fall harvest festival. During this festival, the most elaborate sacrifices of the year were to be offered. Moses recorded the regulations for the sacrifices of these festivals in Numbers chapter 29. The regular daily sacrifices, the New Moon sacrifices that marked the beginning of each month, and the sacrifices for the other festivals of the year are described in Numbers chapter 28. Leviticus chapter 23 contains additional information on these festivals.

Although this was a day of great joy for the people, the text includes an ominous note. It gives the first hint of enemy opposition and the negligence of the people. These factors would delay the completion of the temple for about 20 years.

Beginning the rebuilding of the temple

⁷Then they gave money to the masons and carpenters, and gave food and drink and oil to the people of Sidon and Tyre, so that they would bring cedar logs by sea from Lebanon to Joppa, as authorized by Cyrus king of Persia.

⁸In the second month of the second year after their arrival at the house of God in Jerusalem, Zerubbabel son of Shealtiel, Jeshua son of Jozadak, and the rest of their brothers (the priests and the Levites and all who had returned from the captivity to Jerusalem) began the work, appointing Levites twenty years of age and older to supervise the building of the house of the LORD. ⁹Jeshua and his sons and brothers and Kadmiel and his sons (descendants of Hodaviah) and the sons of Henadad and their sons and brothers—all Levites—joined together in supervising those working on the house of God.

¹⁰When the builders laid the foundation of the temple of the LORD, the priests in their vestments and with trumpets, and the Levites (the sons of Asaph) with cymbals, took their places to praise

the LORD, as prescribed by David king of Israel. ¹¹With praise and thanksgiving they sang to the LORD:

"He is good;
his love to Israel endures forever."

And all the people gave a great shout of praise to the LORD, because the foundation of the house of the LORD was laid. ¹²But many of the older priests and Levites and family heads, who had seen the former temple, wept aloud when they saw the foundation of this temple being laid, while many others shouted for joy. ¹³No one could distinguish the sound of the shouts of joy from the sound of weeping, because the people made so much noise. And the sound was heard far away.

After they had had some time to establish their new homes, the leaders made the necessary arrangements for the rebuilding of the temple. The Jews traded for materials from the Phoenicians, Israel's neighbors to the north in the area that is present-day Lebanon. The Phoenicians had also provided the materials for Solomon's temple. Perhaps some of the hired craftsmen for the new temple were Phoenicians, as they had been at the building of the first temple (1 Kings 5). Because the temple was a house of God, the work was supervised by the Levites, the appointed caretakers of God's house.

The building project began with a special ceremony similar to our groundbreaking or cornerstone laying ceremonies. The ceremony was led by members of the family of Asaph, one of the Levitical families whom David had appointed to be in charge of the temple music (1 Chronicles 25). The words of their song recorded by Ezra are similar to the refrain of Psalm 136 and other psalms. They are apparently just an excerpt from a psalm written or selected for the occasion.

Even though the rebuilding of the temple was an occasion for great joy, some of the old people wept as they remembered the destruction of the first temple. Perhaps their sorrow was caused in part by memories of the nation's sins which had led to the destruction of the first temple and in part by the realization that the poor exiles could not build a temple which would match the riches and outward grandeur of Solomon's temple. As the Lord said through the prophet Haggai, a contemporary of Zerubbabel, "Who of you is left who saw this house in its former glory? How does it look to you now? Does it not seem to you like nothing?" (2:3)

Opposition to the rebuilding

Opposition during the time of Zerubbabel

4 **When the enemies of Judah and Benjamin heard that the exiles were building a temple for the Lord, the God of Israel, ²they came to Zerubbabel and to the heads of the families and said, "Let us help you build because, like you, we seek your God and have been sacrificing to him since the time of Esarhaddon king of Assyria, who brought us here."**

³But Zerubbabel, Jeshua and the rest of the heads of the families of Israel answered, "You have no part with us in building a temple to our God. We alone will build it for the Lord, the God of Israel, as King Cyrus, the king of Persia, commanded us."

⁴Then the peoples around them set out to discourage the people of Judah and make them afraid to go on building. ⁵They hired counselors to work against them and frustrate their plans during the entire reign of Cyrus king of Persia and down to the reign of Darius king of Persia.

The enemies who began to oppose the building of the temple were the Samaritans. They were descendants of people whom the Assyrian kings had imported from Mesopotamia nearly two hundred years earlier to replace the Israelites who had been deported from the Northern

Kingdom in 722 B.C. At that time they had adopted a religion that mixed worship of their heathen gods with worship of the true God. Their worship of the Lord was led by apostate priests provided to them from the Northern Kingdom rather than by true priests from Jerusalem (2 Kings 17:24-41).

The Samaritans had come from many different places in Mesopotamia in several different waves of settlement. They undoubtedly mixed with those Israelites who remained in the land in spite of the deportations. All these factors contributed to the very mixed nature of their religion. It was undoubtedly this mixed worship that influenced the exiles to reject the participation and fellowship of the Samaritans in the rebuilding of the temple. Because they resented this rejection, the Samaritans began to oppose the temple at Jerusalem. This hostility lasted into New Testament times (John 4).

The Samaritans hired men whom we would call "lobbyists" to turn the Persian government against the rebuilding project and to cut off funds. This lobbying continued for about 20 years, throughout the remaining years of Cyrus' reign, through the reigns of Cambyses and Pseudo-Smerdis, who are not mentioned in the Bible, and into the reign of Darius I, which began in 521 B.C.

An example of the enemies' lobbying

⁶At the beginning of the reign of Xerxes, they lodged an accusation against the people of Judah and Jerusalem.

⁷And in the days of Artaxerxes king of Persia, Bishlam, Mithredath, Tabeel and the rest of his associates wrote a letter to Artaxerxes. The letter was written in Aramaic script and in the Aramaic language.

⁸Rehum the commanding officer and Shimshai the secretary wrote a letter against Jerusalem to Artaxerxes the king as follows:

[9]**Rehum the commanding officer and Shimshai the secretary, together with the rest of their associates—the judges and officials over the men from Tripolis, Persia, Erech and Babylon, the Elamites of Susa,** [10]**and other people whom the great and honorable Ashurbanipal deported and settled in the city of Samaria and elsewhere in Trans-Euphrates.**

[11]**(This is a copy of the letter they sent him.)**

To King Artaxerxes,

From your servants, the men of Trans-Euphrates:

[12]**The king should know that the Jews who came up to us from you have gone to Jerusalem and are rebuilding that rebellious and wicked city. They are restoring the walls and repairing the foundations.**

[13]**Furthermore, the king should know that if this city is built and its walls are restored, no more taxes, tribute or duty will be paid, and the royal revenues will suffer.** [14]**Now since we are under obligation to the palace and it is not proper for us to see the king dishonored, we are sending this message to inform the king,** [15]**so that a search may be made in the archives of your predecessors. In these records you will find that this city is a rebellious city, troublesome to kings and provinces, a place of rebellion from ancient times. That is why this city was destroyed.** [16]**We inform the king that if this city is built and its walls are restored, you will be left with nothing in Trans-Euphrates.**

The identities of the two Persian kings in this section have troubled commentators. Ezra chapter 4 clearly describes events that began in the reign of Cyrus. Ezra chapters 5 and 6 report events from the time of Darius I, around 520 B.C., when the building of the temple was completed. We know of no Persian kings named Xerxes or Artaxerxes who reigned between Cyrus and Darius, during the time of Zerubbabel.

Some commentators have tried to explain this difficulty by suggesting that Xerxes and Artaxerxes were alternate names for Cambyses and Pseudo-Smerdis, the kings who ruled between Cyrus and Darius. It is more likely that Ezra here introduces correspondence from a later time, which is nevertheless relevant here because it displays the same hostility shown by the earlier lobbyists in the time of Zerubbabel. Xerxes I was the husband of Esther, who ruled Persia from 486 to 465 B.C. Artaxerxes I (464–423 B.C.) was the king who authorized the returns led by Ezra and Nehemiah. Ezra here uses a letter from his own time, which he had been able to obtain through his connections with the Persian court, as an example of the kind of tactics that had been used by Judah's enemies from the days of Zerubbabel to his own time 60 years later. This interpretation is supported by the fact that this letter refers to the building of the city walls, which was the issue during Ezra's day, rather than to the building of the temple, which was the issue in the time of Zerubbabel.

In their letter the enemies relied on half-truths and flattery to gain their ends. It was true that Judah had been a rebellious nation in the time of the Assyrian and Babylonian Empires, but those days were in the distant past. Because the Persian Empire was constantly plagued by revolts, the enemies knew that the very mention of rebellion was sure to create alarm in Persia. The enemies pretended to be motivated by concern for the king's interests, yet their real motive was jealousy of the people of Jerusalem.

The heading of the letter lists the homes of some of the Samaritans before they had been deported to Israel by Asshurbanipal, a king of Assyria (669–626 B.C.), who had continued the deportation policies of his father Esarhaddon (681–669 B.C.) (Ezra 4:2). There is some uncertainty about the proper translation of some of the titles and place-names in this heading, as a footnote in the NIV indicates. The main difficulty is whether the word "Tripolis" is a place-name or a title. "Persia" may also refer to a class of government officials rather than to the nationality of the settlers. Erech is a city near Babylon, and Susa is in Persia. Trans-Euphrates is the Persian name for the satrapy, or province, that lay west of the Euphrates River. It included Palestine and Syria. Judah was apparently a subdivision of this province.

Ezra 4:8–6:18 is written in Aramaic rather than Hebrew, because Ezra is quoting diplomatic correspondence, which was written in Aramaic. Aramaic served as the international diplomatic language during the Assyrian, Babylonian, and Persian Empires, just as English and French have in modern times.

The king's reply to the enemies

¹⁷**The king sent this reply:**

To Rehum the commanding officer, Shimshai the secretary and the rest of their associates living in Samaria and elsewhere in Trans-Euphrates:

Greetings.

¹⁸**The letter you sent us has been read and translated in my presence. ¹⁹I issued an order and a search was made, and it was found that this city has a long history of revolt against kings and has been a place of rebellion and sedition. ²⁰Jerusalem has had powerful kings ruling over the whole of Trans-Euphrates, and taxes, tribute and duty were paid to them. ²¹Now issue an order to these men to stop work, so that this city will not be rebuilt until I so order. ²²Be careful not to neglect this matter. Why let this threat grow, to the detriment of the royal interests?**

²³**As soon as the copy of the letter of King Artaxerxes was read to Rehum and Shimshai the secretary and their associates, they went immediately to the Jews in Jerusalem and compelled them by force to stop.**

²⁴Thus the work on the house of God in Jerusalem came to a standstill until the second year of the reign of Darius king of Persia.

The letter of Artaxerxes quoted by Ezra indicates that the enemies of Judah were successful in blocking the work of rebuilding Jerusalem in the early years of Artaxerxes before the influence of Ezra and Nehemiah was felt at his court. Ezra uses this letter as an illustration of the methods that had been used by the enemies of Israel to block work on the temple 60 years earlier in the time of Zerubbabel. In the last sentence he alerts the reader that he is now returning to the second year of Darius I (520 B.C.) and resuming the narrative at the point from which he had temporarily digressed in order to introduce the correspondence of Artaxerxes. Ezra 4:6-23 is thus a parenthetical insertion; chronologically verse 24 follows immediately after verse 5.

The temple successfully rebuilt

The help of the prophets

5 **Now Haggai the prophet and Zechariah the prophet, a descendant of Iddo, prophesied to the Jews in Judah and Jerusalem in the name of the God of Israel, who was over them. ²Then Zerubbabel son of Shealtiel and Jeshua son of Jozadak set to work to rebuild the house of God in Jerusalem. And the prophets of God were with them, helping them.**

In the second year of Darius I, nearly 20 years after their return, the Jews still had not completed the building of the temple. The Lord sent two prophets, Haggai and Zechariah, to admonish them for their negligence and to encourage them to complete their work. The messages of these two prophets are recorded in the Old Testament books that bear their names. The book of Haggai is quite short, so you may wish to read it at this point. In it Haggai accused the people of neglecting the reconstruction of the temple because they were too preoccupied with the building up of their own property. He encouraged them with the promise that the glory of this temple would be even greater than the glory of Solomon's temple because the Messiah would appear in this temple and would gather people from all nations to the Lord.

The message of Zechariah is longer and more difficult. The first half of his book contains symbolic visions similar to those in Revelation. The general message of these visions is that the Lord is ruling over the nations and protecting his people. Special words of comfort and encouragement are given to the high priest Jeshua in Zechariah chapters 3 and 6. In the second half of his book, Zechariah delivers several beautiful prophecies about the coming of the Messiah.

When the people heard the words of the Lord spoken through these prophets, they eagerly resumed the work of building God's house.

Letter to Darius

³At that time Tattenai, governor of Trans-Euphrates, and Shethar-Bozenai and their associates went to them and asked, "Who authorized you to rebuild this temple and restore this structure?" ⁴They also asked, "What are the names of the men constructing this building?" ⁵But the eye of their God was watching over the elders of the Jews, and they were not stopped until a report could go to Darius and his written reply be received.

⁶This is a copy of the letter that Tattenai, governor of Trans-Euphrates and Shethar-Bozenai and their associates, the officials of Trans-Euphrates, sent to King Darius. ⁷The report they sent him read as follows:

To King Darius:

Cordial greetings.

[8]The king should know that we went to the district of Judah, to the temple of the great God. The people were building it with large stones and placing the timbers in the walls. The work is being carried on with diligence and is making rapid progress under their direction.

[9]We questioned the elders and asked them, "Who authorized you to rebuild this temple and restore this structure?" [10]We also asked them their names, so that we could write down the names of their leaders for your information.

[11]This is the answer they gave us:

"We are the servants of the God of heaven and earth, and we are rebuilding the temple that was built many years ago, one that a great king of Israel built and finished. [12]But because our fathers angered the God of heaven, he handed them over to Nebuchadnezzar the Chaldean, king of Babylon, who destroyed this temple and deported the people to Babylon.

[13]"However, in the first year of Cyrus king of Babylon, King Cyrus issued a decree to rebuild this house of God. [14]He even removed from the temple of Babylon the gold and silver articles of the house of God, which Nebuchadnezzar had taken from the temple in Jerusalem and brought to the temple in Babylon.

"Then King Cyrus gave them to a man named Sheshbazzar, whom he had appointed governor, [15]and he told him, 'Take these articles and go and deposit them in the temple in Jerusalem. And rebuild the house of God on its site.' [16]So this Sheshbazzar came and laid the foundations of the house of God in Jerusalem. From that day to the present it has been under construction but is not yet finished."

[17]Now if it please the king, let a search be made in the royal archives of Babylon to see if King Cyrus did in fact issue a decree to rebuild this house of God in Jerusalem. Then let the king send us his decision in this matter.

No sooner had the work resumed than renewed opposition threatened to crush the enthusiasm of the people. The project was challenged by Tattenai, the Persian governor of the whole area west of the Euphrates. Judah was apparently a subdivision of the province under his control. Tattenai may have been called to investigate the situation by the enemies of Judah, but Tattenai himself was a fair, conscientious administrator, who carried out his duty in a responsible way. When the Jewish people claimed that their project had been authorized by the Persian government, Tattenai permitted the work to continue until he received verification of their claim from the capital. Apparently, King Cyrus' decree authorizing the Jews to rebuild the temple had been filed away and ignored. Cyrus died eight years after issuing it, and a search had to be made to find the decree.

It was due to God's providence, his eye watching over his people, that the work was able to continue. The Lord had directed the affairs of state in such a way that the Jews at this time were blessed with a fair, impartial ruler so that their new enthusiasm for building God's house was not stifled, and the work was able to progress until a favorable reply was received from the king. Today too it is a great blessing to Christians if they have impartial, conscientious rulers who faithfully carry out their responsibilities and do not hinder God's people from carrying out their responsibilities.

The king's reply

6 **King Darius then issued an order, and they searched in the archives stored in the treasury at Babylon. ²A scroll was found in the citadel of Ecbatana in the province of Media, and this was written on it:**

Memorandum:

³In the first year of King Cyrus, the king issued a decree concerning the temple of God in Jerusalem:

Let the temple be rebuilt as a place to present sacrifices, and let its foundations be laid. It is to be ninety feet high and ninety feet wide, ⁴with three courses of large stones and one of timbers. The costs are to be paid by the royal treasury. ⁵Also, the gold and silver articles of the house of God, which Nebuchadnezzar took from the temple in Jerusalem and brought to Babylon, are to be returned to their places in the temple in Jerusalem; they are to be deposited in the house of God.

⁶Now then, Tattenai, governor of Trans-Euphrates, and Shethar-Bozenai and you, their fellow officials of that province, stay away from there. ⁷Do not interfere with the work on this temple of God. Let the governor of the Jews and the Jewish elders rebuild this house of God on its site.

⁸Moreover, I hereby decree what you are to do for these elders of the Jews in the construction of this house of God:

The expenses of these men are to be fully paid out of the royal treasury, from the revenues of Trans-Euphrates, so that the work will not stop. ⁹Whatever is needed— young bulls, rams, male lambs for burnt offerings to the God of heaven, and wheat, salt, wine and oil, as requested by the priests in Jerusalem—must be given them daily without fail, ¹⁰so that they may offer sacrifices pleasing to the God of heaven and pray for the well-being of the king and his sons.

¹¹Furthermore, I decree that if anyone changes this edict, a beam is to be pulled from his house and he is to be lifted up and impaled on it. And for this crime his house is to be made a pile of rubble. ¹²May God, who has caused his Name to dwell there, overthrow any king or people who lifts a hand to change this decree or to destroy this temple in Jerusalem.

I Darius have decreed it. Let it be carried out with diligence.

If Tattenai's investigation was instigated by Judah's enemies, it certainly backfired on them! Not only did the king authorize the continuation of the building project, but he increased its funding and threatened anyone who interfered. Ezra saw this verdict as an indication of God's providence, as God directs world history for the good of his people.

The way in which the scroll was found in the archives is another example of the providence of God. Apparently, no record of the decree could be found in Babylon, but a detailed version of the decree turned up among records that had been transferred to Ecbatana, the summer residence of the king of Persia (present-day Iran). According to the Old Testament, the Persian government placed a very strong emphasis on precedent, so the discovery of the previous decree virtually assured a favorable verdict for the Jews. Such a verdict was also in keeping with the character of Darius. At this time he was especially eager to promote peace in the empire after the recent civil war in which he had deposed Pseudo-Smerdis.

The ancient world had no concept of the separation of church and state. Everyone expected that the temples and religious rites of the gods of any region should be supported by the tax revenues of that region, in the same way that any other public work would be. If the Lord was the accepted god of Judah, the Persian kings saw nothing unusual about supporting his worship with tax revenues from that area. The rulers also expected the priests to offer prayers and sacrifices for the welfare of the state.

We might be taken aback by the harshness of Darius' decree. It threatened a shameful death and the destruction or confiscation of property for any offender. This was similar to other royal decrees surviving from the ancient Near Eastern empires. Punishment was swift and harsh.

Not only local governors but even great world rulers are under the control of the Lord, the King of kings. Even though their power has been magnified by terrible weapons of mass destruction, the rulers of the world are still under the control of the King of kings. He directs the affairs of this world for the final good of his people.

Completion and dedication of the temple

¹³**Then, because of the decree King Darius had sent, Tattenai, governor of Trans-Euphrates, and Shethar-Bozenai and their associates carried it out with diligence.** ¹⁴**So the elders of the Jews continued to build and prosper under the preaching of Haggai the prophet and Zechariah, a descendant of Iddo. They finished building the temple according to the command of the God of Israel and the decrees of Cyrus, Darius and Artaxerxes, kings of Persia.** ¹⁵**The temple was completed on the third day of the month Adar, in the sixth year of the reign of King Darius.**

¹⁶**Then the people of Israel—the priests, the Levites and the rest of the exiles—celebrated the dedication of the house of God with joy.** ¹⁷**For the dedication of this house of God they offered a hundred bulls, two hundred rams, four hundred male lambs and, as a sin offering for all Israel, twelve male goats, one for each of the tribes of Israel.** ¹⁸**And they installed the priests in their divisions and the Levites in their groups for the service of God at Jerusalem, according to what is written in the Book of Moses.**

The people of Judah successfully completed the temple four years after the beginning of the ministry of Haggai and Zechariah. Ezra's account includes both the spiritual truth that the temple was rebuilt because of the command of God and the political means that God used, namely, the benevolence of the Persian kings. The name of Artaxerxes appears even though the temple was finished well before the beginning of Artaxerxes' rule. Apparently, Ezra did this to compliment his own king and to remind Artaxerxes that he was continuing a policy of benevolence that had ample precedent among his predecessors.

The people dedicated the temple with rejoicing. They were happy to reestablish the way of worship commanded in the Law of Moses. Although most of the returnees were from the tribe of Judah, they offered sacrifices for each tribe to signify the unity of the people of Israel in accordance with such passages as Ezekiel 37:22: "I will make them one nation in the land, . . . and they will never again be two nations or be divided into two kingdoms."

The sacrifices at this dedication are in striking contrast to the magnificent dedication of Solomon's temple. Back then "Solomon offered a sacrifice of fellowship offerings to the LORD: twenty-two thousand cattle and a hundred and twenty thousand sheep and goats" (1 Kings 8:63).

The Passover celebration

¹⁹On the fourteenth day of the first month, the exiles celebrated the Passover. ²⁰The priests and Levites had purified themselves and were all ceremonially clean. The Levites slaughtered the Passover lamb for all the exiles, for their brothers the priests and for themselves. ²¹So the Israelites who had returned from the exile ate it, together with all who had separated themselves from the unclean practices of their Gentile neighbors in order to seek the LORD, the God of Israel. ²²For seven days they celebrated with joy the Feast of Unleavened Bread, because the LORD had filled them with joy by changing the attitude of the king of Assyria, so that he assisted them in the work of the house of God, the God of Israel.

The mention of the Passover is especially significant as a symbol of the full restoration of the Mosaic form of worship. The Passover was the special festival that celebrated the liberation of the Israelites so that they could serve God. There was a further restoration of the unity of the nation when the celebration was joined by people of the land who had separated themselves from their heathen neighbors. It is possible that these people were converts to the Jewish faith, but it is more likely that they were Jews who had remained in the land and mixed with the Samaritans. Now they were returning to the faith of their ancestors.

Critics have often claimed that the reference to the king of Assyria is an obvious mistake and that the king of Persia must be meant. On the contrary, it appears that this is an intentional reference on the part of Ezra. He emphasizes that although Israel's experience with the world empires began with the bitterness of the Assyrian deportations and the Babylonian destruction of the temple, God's grace had changed bitterness to joy. The restoration of the temple was accomplished, and with the help of a heathen king! Ezra's tendency to regard all the world empires as succeeding phases of the same experience is also reflected in 5:13, where Cyrus is called "king of Babylon," and in Nehemiah 9:32, where Israel's whole experience with the three empires of Assyria, Babylon, and Persia is treated as a unit. The vision of world empires in Daniel chapter 2 also treats all the empires as successive phases of the same experience for the people of God.

The first half of the book of Ezra thus closes on a note of joy, triumph, and thanksgiving. The bitterness of exile yields to the joy of being home again, of being able to worship in a restored temple.

Part Two

The Second Return
(7:1–10:44)

The return of Ezra

Ezra comes to Jerusalem

7 **After these things, during the reign of Artaxerxes king of Persia, Ezra son of Seraiah, the son of Azariah, the son of Hilkiah, ²the son of Shallum, the son of Zadok, the son of Ahitub, ³the son of Amariah, the son of Azariah, the son of Meraioth, ⁴the son of Zerahiah, the son of Uzzi, the son of Bukki, ⁵the son of Abishua, the son of Phinehas, the son of Eleazar, the son of Aaron the chief priest—⁶this Ezra came up from Babylon. He was a teacher well versed in the Law of Moses, which the LORD, the God of Israel, had given. The king had granted him everything he asked, for the hand of the LORD his God was on him. ⁷Some of the Israelites, including priests, Levites, singers, gatekeepers and temple servants, also came up to Jerusalem in the seventh year of King Artaxerxes.**

⁸Ezra arrived in Jerusalem in the fifth month of the seventh year of the king. ⁹He had begun his journey from Babylon on the first day of the first month, and he arrived in Jerusalem on the first day of the fifth month, for the gracious hand of his God was on him. ¹⁰For Ezra had devoted himself to the study and observance of the Law of the LORD, and to teaching its decrees and laws in Israel.

The book of Ezra resumes in 457 B.C., the seventh year of Artaxerxes, about 55 years after the completion of the temple under Zerubbabel. The events recorded in the book of Esther occurred during this interval.

The main purpose of this section is to introduce us to Ezra. His genealogy is given to show that Ezra was a member of the family which provided the high priests for Israel. Like many biblical genealogies, Ezra's genealogy skips some generations. It omits six names that appear in the corresponding genealogy in 1 Chronicles chapter 6 and may have other gaps as well. In biblical genealogies "son" sometimes means grandson, great-grandson, or an even more remote relationship.

Seraiah was the name of the last high priest in Jerusalem before the Babylonian Captivity (1 Chronicles 6:14). Jeshua, the high priest when the temple was rebuilt, was Seraiah's grandson. So if the Seraiah in our text is the same Seraiah, we have a time span of over 120 years between Seraiah and his "son" Ezra. Ezra was probably his great-grandson or even great-great-grandson. The point of the genealogy, then, is not to list every ancestor of Ezra but to establish Ezra's credentials as a member of the family that had supplied Israel's high priests throughout its history.

Ezra's ability and character provided even more important credentials for his role as a reformer. He was a well trained, learned teacher of God's law. He didn't just study the law as a scholar, but he observed it as a believing child of God. Ezra was a good teacher because his thorough knowledge and devotion to teaching were coupled with his godly life. He taught others by example as well as by words.

Ezra provides a good example for all of us, whether we teach God's Word as pastors, Christian elementary school teachers, Sunday school teachers, parents teaching our own children, or Christians teaching our neighbors by our example. To be effective teachers or examples, we need a correct and thorough knowledge of God's Word. This comes only through the regular lifelong reading and studying of God's

Word. We can never graduate from our need to study God's Word in daily Bible reading and in regular Bible classes. Yet Bible knowledge by itself is not enough. We need faith and love worked by the gospel. Such love motivates us to try to keep God's law and to share God's Word with others. Then we are not only hearers of the Word, but like Ezra, we become doers and teachers as well. May God so bless our study of his Word!

This brings us to Ezra's most important asset as a helper of God's people. It is found in the repeated phrase "the hand of the LORD his God was on him." Ezra had all the credentials and ability, but he could succeed only if God blessed his efforts. The same is true for us. Our efforts, no matter how wisely planned or how well-intentioned they may be, can only succeed with God's blessing. We should work hard for the gospel. But we humbly depend upon God to bless our efforts with success through the power of his Holy Spirit.

King Artaxerxes' letter to Ezra

¹¹**This is a copy of the letter King Artaxerxes had given to Ezra the priest and teacher, a man learned in matters concerning the commands and decrees of the LORD for Israel:**

¹²**Artaxerxes, king of kings,**

To Ezra the priest, a teacher of the Law of the God of heaven:

Greetings.

¹³**Now I decree that any of the Israelites in my kingdom, including priests and Levites, who wish to go to Jerusalem with you, may go. ¹⁴You are sent by the king and his seven advisers to inquire about Judah and Jerusalem with regard to the Law of your God, which is in your hand. ¹⁵Moreover, you are to take with you the silver and gold that the king**

and his advisers have freely given to the God of Israel, whose dwelling is in Jerusalem, ¹⁶together with all the silver and gold you may obtain from the province of Babylon, as well as the freewill offerings of the people and priests for the temple of their God in Jerusalem. ¹⁷With this money be sure to buy bulls, rams and male lambs, together with their grain offerings and drink offerings, and sacrifice them on the altar of the temple of your God in Jerusalem.

¹⁸You and your brother Jews may then do whatever seems best with the rest of the silver and gold, in accordance with the will of your God. ¹⁹Deliver to the God of Jerusalem all the articles entrusted to you for worship in the temple of your God. ²⁰And anything else needed for the temple of your God that you may have occasion to supply, you may provide from the royal treasury.

²¹Now I, King Artaxerxes, order all the treasurers of Trans-Euphrates to provide with diligence whatever Ezra the priest, a teacher of the Law of the God of heaven, may ask of you—²²up to a hundred talents of silver, a hundred cors of wheat, a hundred baths of wine, a hundred baths of olive oil, and salt without limit. ²³Whatever the God of heaven has prescribed, let it be done with diligence for the temple of the God of heaven. Why should there be wrath against the realm of the king and of his sons? ²⁴You are also to know that you have no authority to impose taxes, tribute or duty on any of the priests, Levites, singers, gatekeepers, temple servants or other workers at this house of God.

²⁵And you, Ezra, in accordance with the wisdom of your God, which you possess, appoint magistrates and judges to administer justice to all the people of Trans-Euphrates—all who know the laws of your God. And you are to teach any who do not know them. ²⁶Whoever does not obey the law of your God and the law of the king must surely be punished by death, banishment, confiscation of property, or imprisonment.

This letter contains many similarities to the letter of Darius in chapter 6, so the comments made there need not be repeated here. Like the earlier letters, this one is also in Aramaic. The king gave Ezra a financial grant and the authorization to raise additional funds through contributions from the Jews in Babylon and Judah. Ezra's mission was thus given the status of an official inspection tour on behalf of the Persian government.

The final section of the letter gave Ezra authority to govern the Jews of Trans-Euphrates, not only by the laws of the Persian Empire but by the Mosaic Law as well. Ezra was not the governor of the entire province of Trans-Euphrates. He had authority only over the Jews as a semiautonomous national group within the province.

Artaxerxes was very generous to Ezra, but his generosity had limits. The section of the letter addressed to the treasurers of Trans-Euphrates set limits on the amount of provisions Ezra could withdraw from the warehouses. These directions are very similar to stipulations contained in the traveling credentials of other Persian officials, such as the Arsham correspondence found in Egypt.

It is often difficult to translate ancient measurements into our modern equivalents. A cor is probably equal to between four to six bushels, and a bath to about six gallons. The talent is especially difficult to translate because it was not always the same. To further complicate matters there was a light talent and a heavy one, which was double the weight of the light. The talent referred to by Ezra was probably about 66 pounds. Therefore, the amounts allotted by the king were more than three tons of silver, six hundred bushels of grain, and six hundred gallons of wine. It should be remembered that these measurements are approximations.

Ezra's response to the letter

27Praise be to the Lord, the God of our fathers, who has put it into the king's heart to bring honor to the house of the Lord in

Jerusalem in this way ²⁸and who has extended his good favor to me before the king and his advisers and all the king's powerful officials. Because the hand of the LORD my God was on me, I took courage and gathered leading men from Israel to go up with me.

For the third time in this chapter, we read that the hand of God was on Ezra, blessing his efforts with success. Apparently, Ezra had appeared before the Persian court to argue his case for his mission to Jerusalem. When he received a favorable verdict from the king and cabinet, he recognized this as a blessing from God. Ezra could plead the case, but it was only God who could move the heart of the king. The book of Proverbs makes this very clear: "To man belong the plans of the heart, but from the LORD comes the reply of the tongue. Commit to the LORD whatever you do, and your plans will succeed. The king's heart is in the hand of the LORD; he directs it like a watercourse wherever he pleases" (16:1,3; 21:1).

The list of those returning with Ezra

8 These are the family heads and those registered with them who came up with me from Babylon during the reign of King Artaxerxes:

> ²**of the descendants of Phinehas, Gershom;**
> **of the descendants of Ithamar, Daniel;**
> **of the descendants of David, Hattush ³of the descendants of Shecaniah;**
> **of the descendants of Parosh, Zechariah, and with him were registered 150 men;**
> ⁴**of the descendants of Pahath-Moab, Eliehoenai son of Zerahiah, and with him 200 men;**
> ⁵**of the descendants of Zattu, Shecaniah son of Jahaziel, and with him 300 men;**

⁶of the descendants of Adin, Ebed son of Jonathan, and
with him 50 men;
⁷of the descendants of Elam, Jeshaiah son of Athaliah, and
with him 70 men;
⁸of the descendants of Shephatiah, Zebadiah son of
Michael, and with him 80 men;
⁹of the descendants of Joab, Obadiah son of Jehiel, and
with him 218 men;
¹⁰of the descendants of Bani, Shelomith son of Josiphiah,
and with him 160 men;
¹¹of the descendants of Bebai, Zechariah son of Bebai, and
with him 28 men;
¹²of the descendants of Azgad, Johanan son of Hakkatan,
and with him 110 men;
¹³of the descendants of Adonikam, the last ones, whose
names were Eliphelet, Jeuel and Shemaiah, and with
them 60 men;
¹⁴of the descendants of Bigvai, Uthai and Zaccur, and with
them 70 men.

Like the lists in Ezra chapter 2, this list of returnees is
intended to emphasize the grace of God. The Lord preserved the people of Israel during their exile so that they
would be able to return to the Promised Land.

The first two men listed were heads of priestly families
descended from Aaron. Phinehas was a grandson of Aaron;
Ithamar was Aaron's youngest son. The third person listed,
Hattush, was from the royal house of David. These three
men emphasized the restoration of Davidic and Aaronic
leadership for Israel. The names of these three leaders are
followed by a list of 12 groups of returnees with their leaders.
The same family names appear in the list of those who
returned under Zerubbabel in Ezra chapter 2.

The fact that 12 groups are listed might have been a
coincidence, but it was probably a deliberate representation of the 12 tribes of Israel. Moreover, it symbolized the

reunification of the nation under the leadership appointed by God. Ezekiel 37:15-28 indicates the importance that this reunification under Davidic leadership had for the people in exile. "I will make them one nation in the land," promised God (verse 22).

The unity of God's people under the priests and kings reached its fullness when Christ, the son of David and our Great High Priest, came and gathered all believers, whether Jews or Gentiles, into one church. The strong emphasis on family ties and continuity with preceding generations that Ezra's lists express reminds us to appreciate our adoption into God's family. We have ties with the generations of believers who have gone before us.

Gathering the people

[15]I assembled them at the canal that flows toward Ahava, and we camped there three days. When I checked among the people and the priests, I found no Levites there. [16]So I summoned Eliezer, Ariel, Shemaiah, Elnathan, Jarib, Elnathan, Nathan, Zechariah and Meshullam, who were leaders, and Joiarib and Elnathan, who were men of learning, [17]and I sent them to Iddo, the leader in Casiphia. I told them what to say to Iddo and his kinsmen, the temple servants in Casiphia, so that they might bring attendants to us for the house of our God. [18]Because the gracious hand of our God was on us, they brought us Sherebiah, a capable man, from the descendants of Mahli son of Levi, the son of Israel, and Sherebiah's sons and brothers, 18 men; [19]and Hashabiah, together with Jeshaiah from the descendants of Merari, and his brothers and nephews, 20 men. [20]They also brought 220 of the temple servants—a body that David and the officials had established to assist the Levites. All were registered by name.

Ezra summoned the returnees to a camp at one of the canals flowing off the Euphrates River near Babylon. There they prepared for the journey. If the numbers in the preceding list are the full count of those returning to Jerusalem, the group numbered only a couple thousand, a much smaller return than that at the time of Zerubbabel.

Ezra was especially disappointed by the lack of turnout of Levites. He was planning reform of the temple services and needed temple workers if he was to be successful. Perhaps the temple workers were unwilling to leave their established homes in Babylon in order to perform what seemed to them to be menial tasks in the temple. At any rate, Ezra found it necessary to send a delegation of leaders to recruit temple workers. They were successful in obtaining workers from Casiphia, apparently a town or place of worship where there was a concentration of Levites. Ezra again credited his success to the helping hand of God.

Notice that the narration here has switched to the first person, "I." This indicates that Ezra's personal memoirs or recollections are the source of this part of the book.

Preparations for the journey

²¹**There, by the Ahava Canal, I proclaimed a fast, so that we might humble ourselves before our God and ask him for a safe journey for us and our children, with all our possessions. ²²I was ashamed to ask the king for soldiers and horsemen to protect us from enemies on the road, because we had told the king, "The gracious hand of our God is on everyone who looks to him, but his great anger is against all who forsake him." ²³So we fasted and petitioned our God about this, and he answered our prayer.**

²⁴**Then I set apart twelve of the leading priests, together with Sherebiah, Hashabiah and ten of their brothers, ²⁵and I weighed out to them the offering of silver and gold and the articles that the king, his advisers, his officials and all Israel present there had donated for the house of God. ²⁶I weighed out to them 650 talents of silver, silver articles weighing 100 talents, 100 talents of gold,**

²⁷**20 bowls of gold valued at 1,000 darics, and two fine articles of polished bronze, as precious as gold.**

²⁸**I said to them, "You as well as these articles are consecrated to the L**ORD**. The silver and gold are a freewill offering to the L**ORD**, the God of your fathers. ²⁹Guard them carefully until you weigh them out in the chambers of the house of the L**ORD** in Jerusalem before the leading priests and Levites and the family heads of Israel." ³⁰Then the priests and Levites received the silver and gold and sacred articles that had been weighed out to be taken to the house of our God in Jerusalem.**

Ezra made two necessary preparations for the journey. First, he sought God's protection, since their convoy loaded with treasures would have provided an ideal target for bandits, raiders, or unscrupulous officials along the way. Considering that a talent was more than 60 pounds, the amounts of gold and silver entrusted to the group was indeed fantastic in comparison with the availability of these precious metals today. Because Ezra had spoken confidently of the Lord's power to the king, he was unwilling to ask for a military escort. Ezra resolved to depend entirely on the care of God. The assembled group therefore sought such help in fervent prayer.

Second, for the safekeeping of the royal gifts and so that there would be no suspicion that any of the money had been diverted to improper use, Ezra provided for a full inventory of the gifts and for trustees to be responsible for the administration of the finances. We should use the same care in the administration of the church's financial affairs today. Like Ezra, we will want to avoid loss or any suspicion of the misuse of funds, which would be very harmful to the reputation of the church and an offense to the givers. Saint Paul provides us with an example of the same carefulness and concern in the New Testament. Speaking of a donation to be sent to the poor, Paul remarks: "As we carry the offering, . . . we want to avoid any criticism of the way we administer this liberal gift. For we are taking pains to do what is right, not only in the eyes of the Lord but also in the eyes of men" (2 Corinthians 8:19-21).

The arrival in Jerusalem

³¹On the twelfth day of the first month we set out from the Ahava Canal to go to Jerusalem. The hand of our God was on us, and he protected us from enemies and bandits along the way. ³²So we arrived in Jerusalem, where we rested three days.

³³On the fourth day, in the house of our God, we weighed out the silver and gold and the sacred articles into the hands of Meremoth son of Uriah, the priest. Eleazer son of Phinehas was with him, and so were the Levites Jozabad son of Jeshua and Noadiah son of Binnui. ³⁴Everything was accounted for by number and weight, and the entire weight was recorded at that time.

³⁵Then the exiles who had returned from captivity sacrificed burnt offerings to the God of Israel: twelve bulls for all Israel, ninety-six rams, seventy-seven male lambs and, as a sin offering, twelve male goats. All this was a burnt offering to the LORD. ³⁶They also delivered the king's orders to the royal satraps and to the governors of Trans-Euphrates, who then gave assistance to the people and to the house of God.

The Lord brought Ezra and his group safely to Jerusalem. Including the 12 days of preparation by the Ahava Canal, the journey from Babylon to Jerusalem lasted four months, from the beginning of spring until midsummer (7:9). It was only five hundred miles from Babylon to Jerusalem as the crow flies, but it was about nine hundred miles by the caravan route that passed around the desert to the north (see the map entitled "The return from exile," page 199). If we assume that Ezra's group did not travel on the Sabbath, they had to walk an average of 12 miles a day. One of Ezra's favorite phrases, "the hand of our God was on us," explains how the people were kept safe during this long, tiring journey.

After their arrival in Jerusalem, Ezra and the people promptly fulfilled three responsibilities. They delivered the offerings to the appropriate officials at the temple, and everything was fully accounted for. They offered sacrifices for themselves and all the people of Israel. And they delivered their orders from the king to the Persian officials, who now cooperated fully with them.

At last, the exiles were home in Jerusalem. Once again, they had the joy of worshiping in the temple. Their trip seemed to be a great success. But the joy was not to last. Ezra soon came face-to-face with a serious problem that threatened the very future of Israel.

The problem of intermarriage

Ezra learns of the problem

9 **After these things had been done, the leaders came to me and said, "The people of Israel, including the priests and Levites, have not kept themselves separate from the neighboring peoples with their detestable practices, like those of the Canaanites, Hittites, Perizzites, Jebusites, Ammonites, Moabites, Egyptians and Amorites. ²They have taken some of their daughters as wives for themselves and their sons, and have mingled the holy race with the people around them. And the leaders and officials have led the way in this unfaithfulness."**

³When I heard this, I tore my tunic and cloak, pulled hair from my head and beard and sat down appalled. ⁴Then everyone who trembled at the words of the God of Israel gathered around me because of this unfaithfulness of the exiles. And I sat there appalled until the evening sacrifice.

It is not clear exactly when Ezra found out about the problem of intermarriage. Ezra chapter 10 indicates that the meeting to deal with the problem took place about four months after Ezra's arrival in Jerusalem. Perhaps it took several months for Ezra to find out about the problem because he was out of town, presenting his orders to the Persian officials. Or perhaps he was so busy getting his work organized that he did not realize what was going on around him.

At any rate, when Ezra heard about the relapse into mixed marriages, he was shocked. He openly demonstrated his grief and dismay with the emotional signs of mourning that were customary in his culture; Ezra tore his clothing and disfigured his hair and beard. To people of our culture who aren't shocked by much of anything anymore, Ezra's behavior may seem like an overreaction. Why was he so shocked and grief-stricken by the report of intermarriage with the neighboring peoples?

For one thing, the Lord Almighty had prohibited intermarriage with the peoples of Canaan. Exodus 34:10-16 and Deuteronomy 7:1-11 are two of the many passages that forbid this practice. God's command was unmistakably clear, "Do not intermarry with them" (Deuteronomy 7:3). The motive for banning marriage with the people of Canaan was not racial, but religious. The Israelites had been set aside as God's chosen people, not because of any superiority on their part but so that the true worship of God could be preserved in at least one little corner of the world until the promised Savior would come and deliver the gospel to the whole world. God called Israel "the holy race," or literally "a holy seed," because the promised Savior was to be born as the descendant of Abraham and David.

To keep the Israelites separate from the heathen nations, God had given them the ceremonial law, which regulated their diet and many other aspects of their daily life. These regulations made Israel's way of life very different from that of the peoples around it and served as a kind of fence, or barrier, to keep the Jews separated from surrounding peoples. The people of Israel would also be different than their neighbors if they observed the principles of God's moral law as summarized in the Ten Commandments. If, however, the Israelites mixed with the heathen peoples who surrounded them, there was a great danger of losing their distinctness.

Mixing with the heathen was like playing with fire because of the temptation to follow the abominable practices of the Canaanite religion. Not only did this idolatrous religion lack any knowledge of the true God, but it embraced the grossest kinds of immorality as part of its worship. Sexual immorality and human sacrifice, especially of children, were acts of worship in the Canaanite religion. The Canaanites practiced every form of sexual immorality. Leviticus chapters 18 and 20 and Numbers chapter 25 mention the abominable practices of the Canaanites, which included incest and bestiality. There is not much evidence to indicate how widely such rites were practiced in Palestine at Ezra's time, but there is considerable evidence that similar religious practices continued in North Africa and Asia Minor until New Testament times.

Even if the Jews who intermarried with the surrounding peoples did not engage in the most terrible forms of idolatry, they were nevertheless guilty of direct disobedience of God's command. And they were endangering the existence of Israel as a distinct people from whom the Savior would come.

What made the matter even more shocking was the fact that Israel's mixed marriages had been a chief cause of the disastrous Assyrian and Babylonian captivities. The people of Israel had been through the judgment of destruction and captivity. Now they had experienced the joy of restoration to their land. But they still had not learned their lesson. To make matters even worse, the spiritual leaders of the people, who should have been leading them in the right way, were ringleaders in defying God's law. No wonder Ezra was shocked and appalled!

Those who "trembled" at God's Word gathered themselves to Ezra. Would we place ourselves into this group? Many people today have not only lost a fear of judgment but even a sense of responsibility for their own sins. Even Christians have been so exposed to violence and immorality, especially through the entertainment media, that what would have shocked us a few decades ago hardly causes us to raise an eyebrow today.

No matter how commonplace sin becomes, it should still shock us. For no matter how much society may condone it, every infraction of God's law is still an offense against a holy God, who has vowed to punish every sin. The holy God cannot stand evil in his presence; he still hates every sin and threatens every sinner with eternal damnation. Although we are offered free forgiveness through Christ, we never dare to think lightly of sin or underestimate its consequences. We enjoy forgiveness only because Christ suffered the terrible penalty of sin and endured God's wrath for us on the cross. While many no longer tremble at God's law, we need to be awakened to the seriousness of sin by the strong words of God's law. We need to work to restore a fear of the holy wrath of God in a society that is increasingly calloused to sin.

Confessing the guilt of the nation

⁵Then, at the evening sacrifice, I rose from my self-abasement, with my tunic and cloak torn, and fell on my knees with my hands spread out to the LORD my God ⁶and prayed:

"O my God, I am too ashamed and disgraced to lift up my face to you, my God, because our sins are higher than

our heads and our guilt has reached to the heavens. ⁷From the days of our forefathers until now, our guilt has been great. Because of our sins, we and our kings and our priests have been subjected to the sword and captivity, to pillage and humiliation at the hand of foreign kings, as it is today.

One of the surprising things about Ezra's reaction is the intensity of his shame and grief. He feels "ashamed and disgraced" for the sins of his nation, even though he himself was not guilty of the sin of intermarriage. In our day, when many feel little responsibility even for their own sins, it strikes us as strange that anyone would feel such personal guilt and pain over the sins of others. A more common reaction might be a feeling of smug satisfaction, like that of the Pharisee who thanked God that he was not as sinful as the tax collector (Luke 18:9-14). Political leaders today seldom feel compelled to resign because of the misdeeds of their subordinates as they once did. They might be more inclined to put the blame for their own misdeeds on their subordinates and sacrifice the subordinates to save themselves.

Ezra's sense of responsibility for the sins of others might seem peculiar to us. Yet it was an appropriate reaction. This becomes clear when we remember that God's people are an organism that works like the human body. "The body is a unit, though it is made up of many parts; . . . Now you are the body of Christ, and each one of you is a part of it" (1 Corinthians 12:12,27). When you have a headache or stomachache, your whole body can be so incapacitated that you cannot perform your daily work. Poison that enters the body through a wound in the foot can kill the whole body. In the same way, when part of the nation of Israel defied God's law, the whole nation suffered the devastating consequences of that sin, namely, captivity to heathen nations. Today too when a member of Christ's body, the church, falls into a grievous sin, the work of the whole church can suffer. When unrepented sin is ignored, the poison can spread to other members of the body.

Like Ezra, we should feel grief, not smugness, when fellow Christians fall into sin. Like Ezra and like Moses at the time of the golden calf (Exodus 32), we should intercede for our fellow Christians at the throne of grace, praying that God will grant them repentance. We should also pray for our nation, so that the drift into moral indifference and self-centeredness will be halted by the clear words of God's law. If the people of a nation live in reckless disregard for God's law, the whole nation will ultimately pay the price. It will not only be the fault of others "out there" somewhere. We too will share the blame.

We are indeed our brothers' keepers. We are involved and responsible. Interceding for others before the God of mercy is one of the most important ways of fulfilling our Christian responsibility. We need a heartfelt compassion and concern regarding the sins of others so that we never close our eyes through smugness or indifference. Instead, we will pray for them and confront them with God's Word.

Acknowledging God's undeserved mercy

8"But now, for a brief moment, the LORD our God has been gracious in leaving us a remnant and giving us a firm place in his sanctuary, and so our God gives light to our eyes and a little relief in our bondage. 9Though we are slaves, our God has not deserted us in our bondage. He has shown us kindness in the sight of the kings of Persia: He has granted us new life to rebuild the house of our God and repair its ruins, and he has given us a wall of protection in Judah and Jerusalem.

At the time of Moses, the Israelites had promised, "Everything the LORD has said we will do" (Exodus 24:3).

Under Moses' successor, Joshua, the nation again committed itself, "We will serve the LORD our God and obey him" (Joshua 24:24). Yet over and over again, Israel broke its promises to remain faithful to God. In spite of such unfaithfulness on the part of his people, the Lord remained faithful to his promise to bring the Savior into the world through that nation of Israel.

God brought a remnant of Israel back to Jerusalem. He allowed the restoration of the temple worship under the leadership of priests descended from Aaron. He restored political leadership to the family of David. He protected the people from the enemies who surrounded them in the land. The Jews' political freedom was not complete; they still had to pay taxes and observe the decrees of the Persian kings. But because of the favor of the Persian kings, the Israelites enjoyed religious freedom through the reestablishment of temple worship.

Being torn away from the temple worship in Jerusalem had been the greatest pain of the captivity. The psalmist expressed this bitter grief:

> By the rivers of Babylon we sat and wept
>> when we remembered Zion.
> There on the poplars
>> we hung our harps,
> for there our captors asked us for songs,
>> our tormentors demanded songs of joy;
>> they said, "Sing us one of the songs of Zion!"
> How can we sing the songs of the LORD
>> while in a foreign land?
> If I forget you, O Jerusalem,
>> may my right hand forget its skill.
> May my tongue cling to the roof of my mouth
>> if I do not remember you,

if I do not consider Jerusalem
my highest joy. (Psalm 137:1-6)

No other spot on earth could substitute for Jerusalem, the site chosen by God as the place where the Old Testament sacrifices had to be performed. Now the Israelites were home again in Jerusalem, offering the prescribed sacrifices in the temple and waiting for the Savior to come. God's people could truly claim to be free, even though their political freedom was not complete. Believers have that priceless freedom which comes through God's Word and the Savior. As Jesus said, "If you hold to my teaching, you are really my disciples. Then you will know the truth, and the truth will set you free" (John 8:31,32). Freedom from sin, death, and Satan's power—this is the greatest liberty of all!

The nation had truly come back from the dead, as Ezekiel had prophesied (37:1-14). Surely after all this, Israel would gladly serve and obey the Lord. What excuse could there be for despising God's commands?

Confessing the nation's continued sin

¹⁰"But now, O our God, what can we say after this? For we have disregarded the commands ¹¹you gave through your servants the prophets when you said: 'The land you are entering to possess is a land polluted by the corruption of its peoples. By their detestable practices they have filled it with their impurity from one end to the other. ¹²Therefore, do not give your daughters in marriage to their sons or take their daughters for your sons. Do not seek a treaty of friendship with them at any time, that you may be strong and eat the good things of the land and leave it to your children as an everlasting inheritance.'

¹³"What has happened to us is a result of our evil deeds and our great guilt, and yet, our God, you have punished us less than our sins deserved and have given us a remnant like this. ¹⁴Shall we again break your commands and intermarry

with the peoples who commit such detestable practices? Would you not be angry enough with us to destroy us, leaving no remnant or survivor? ¹⁵**O LORD, God of Israel, you are righteous! We are left this day as a remnant. Here we are before you in our guilt, though because of it not one of us can stand in your presence."**

The facts were clear. Israel had no excuse. There was no doubt that Israel had flagrantly despised God's law. Ezra demonstrated this by repeating the warning God had given his people. Ezra's quotation of God's warning is not an exact quotation of a specific Old Testament passage. Rather, it is a summary of many passages.

Most of the language of Ezra's summary is adapted from the book of Deuteronomy. That whole book consists of Moses' farewell sermons to Israel. These sermons warn of the terrible consequences of disobeying God's law and promise blessings for those who obey. Many other prophets had repeated the warnings first given by Moses. But Israel disregarded the warnings and scorned the promises. The people went their own way. Truly Ezra could say, "You have punished us less than our sins deserved." Because of his mercy and his gospel promise, God had forgiven their sins and reestablished a remnant of the nation. Incredible as it seems, in the face of all God's goodness and mercy, the nation of Israel had returned to the same sin that had been its downfall in the past!

Who can comprehend the foolishness and blindness of sin? We must agree with the lament of Jeremiah: "The heart is deceitful above all things and beyond cure. Who can understand it?" (17:9). We are shocked by the stubbornness of Israel, but Ezra could pray this prayer for us too. We would do well to take his words on our own lips: "You have punished us less than our sins deserve and shown us your mercy. Shall we again break your commands?" How often we repeat the same sins over and over again, even though those sins bring grief to us and to others! How often we do things we know are wrong! How often we neglect things we know we should do! Yet God for Christ's sake graciously forgives us, so that we can rejoice as David did:

> Praise the LORD, O my soul,
> and forget not all his benefits—
> he does not treat us as our sins deserve
> or repay us according to our iniquities.
> As far as the east is from the west,
> so far has he removed our transgressions from us.
> Praise the LORD, O my soul. (Psalm 103:2,10,12,22)

The people join Ezra in repentance

10 While Ezra was praying and confessing, weeping and throwing himself down before the house of God, a large crowd of Israelites—men, women and children—gathered around him. They too wept bitterly. ²Then Shecaniah son of Jehiel, one of the descendants of Elam, said to Ezra, "We have been unfaithful to our God by marrying foreign women from the peoples around us. But in spite of this, there is still hope for Israel. ³Now let us make a covenant before our God to send away all these women and their children, in accordance with the counsel of my lord and of those who fear the commands of our God. Let it be done according to the Law. ⁴Rise up; this matter is in your hands. We will support you, so take courage and do it."

⁵So Ezra rose up and put the leading priests and Levites and all Israel under oath to do what had been suggested. And they took the oath. ⁶Then Ezra withdrew from before the house of God and went to the room of Jehohanan son of Eliashib. While he was there, he ate no food and drank no water, because he continued to mourn over the unfaithfulness of the exiles.

Ezra continued his mourning because of the sin of the exiles, but a ray of hope emerged when faithful people from among the exiles joined him in his grief. They shared Ezra's dismay at Israel's relapse into the sin of intermarriage with the people of the land and encouraged him to take action to correct the situation. Shecaniah, who served as their spokesman, ably summarized the situation. By intermarrying with the surrounding nations, the people had treacherously broken their covenant with the Lord.

Nevertheless, the situation was not hopeless. In passages like Deuteronomy 30:1-10, God had promised forgiveness and restoration to Israel if those who had broken the covenant would repent and return to him. Solomon had held out the same hope in his prayer at the dedication of the temple (1 Kings 8:46-53). Ultimately, this hope of forgiveness depended upon the promised Messiah. The Lord would preserve his people so that this promise could be fulfilled. He could forgive his people because their sins would be paid for by the coming Savior. This hope brought light into a dark situation. It gave the people courage.

It must have been a great comfort to Ezra to know he did not stand alone. Even a man as staunch as the prophet Elijah lost heart when he thought he stood alone against the idolatry of Ahab and Jezebel (1 Kings 19). Pastors, teachers, and other leaders called by God need the encouragement of fellow Christians when they face the difficult and often unpopular task of rebuking or disciplining the impenitent. Let us make every effort to give such support to faithful leaders, just as Shecaniah and his companions did in the past. Encouraged by the people's support, Ezra took decisive action to deal with the problem. And with Ezra behind them, the leaders vowed to correct the situation.

Ezra withdrew to fast and mourn while awaiting the outcome. His sorrow would not end until the situation had been corrected.

Dealing with the sin

7A proclamation was then issued throughout Judah and Jerusalem for all the exiles to assemble in Jerusalem. 8Anyone who failed to appear within three days would forfeit all his property, in accordance with the decision of the officials and elders, and would himself be expelled from the assembly of the exiles.

9Within the three days, all the men of Judah and Benjamin had gathered in Jerusalem. And on the twentieth day of the ninth month, all the people were sitting in the square before the house of God, greatly distressed by the occasion and because of the rain. 10Then Ezra the priest stood up and said to them, "You have been unfaithful; you have married foreign women, adding to Israel's guilt. 11Now make confession to the LORD, the God of your fathers, and do his will. Separate yourselves from the people around you and from your foreign wives."

12The whole assembly responded with a loud voice: "You are right! We must do as you say. 13But there are many people here and it is the rainy season; so we cannot stand outside. Besides, this matter cannot be taken care of in a day or two, because we have sinned greatly in this thing. 14Let our officials act for the whole assembly. Then let everyone in our towns who has married a foreign woman come at a set time, along with the elders and judges of each town, until the fierce anger of our God in this matter is turned away from us." 15Only Jonathan son of Asahel and Jahzeiah son of Tikvah, supported by Meshullam and Shabbethai the Levite, opposed this.

16So the exiles did as was proposed. Ezra the priest selected men who were family heads, one from each family division, and all of them designated by name. On the first day of the tenth month they sat down to investigate the cases, 17and by the first day of the first month they finished dealing with all the men who had married foreign women.

All Israel was summoned to deal with the situation. Ezra's commission from King Artaxerxes gave him authority to deal with the sin of intermarriage and to impose harsh penalties (7:26), but he worked through the local officials of Jerusalem and Judah. In this way his actions would have broader support than if he had acted on his own. The removal of the offense would be achieved in the most harmonious way if it was based on the agreement of the whole congregation rather than imposed by Ezra acting alone. Ezra's approach was successful. The overwhelming majority of the people supported the decision to end the practice of intermarriage with the heathen.

According to the NIV translation, Jonathan, Jahzeiah, Meshullam, and Shabbethai were the only men to oppose any action to correct the situation. The verse in question is somewhat ambiguous in Hebrew, so it is not completely clear what each of these men was supporting or opposing. Some commentators have interpreted the verse to mean that Jonathan and Jahzeiah were zealous supporters of Ezra who were opposed to any *delay* of the action. It seems more likely, however, that these four men were the only ones to oppose action against the illegal marriages. According to this interpretation, everyone else favored action but agreed that it would take some time to solve the problem. There is nothing in the text to suggest that Ezra had any objection to the proposed delay.

The reason for the delay was twofold. It was midwinter, when cold rain falls almost every day in Israel. The time was hardly right for mass outdoor meetings. Furthermore, the problem was simply too big to deal with in a day. The large number of people involved in this offense could be dealt with most effectively if each individual was confronted by a group of elders who would serve as representatives of the whole assembly. In some ways, this was similar to our proceedings in church discipline today. Congregations have elders who assist the pastor in dealing with discipline cases on behalf of the whole congregation. When the people followed this procedure, within three months they had dealt with all the cases.

At first glance, it may seem that this approach added one sin to another. One might ask, "Didn't the proposed solution require sending away their heathen wives and families, thereby adding the sin of divorce to the previous sin of intermarriage?" In 1 Corinthians chapter 7, Saint Paul tells New Testament believers who are married to unbelievers to remain married to their unbelieving husbands or wives, as long as the husband or wife is willing. In reality, the two cases are quite different. For one thing, the people in Corinth had married heathen spouses while they themselves were still heathen. As Gentiles, they had been under no command of God forbidding intermarriage but had entered those marriages in good faith. The situation was quite different in Ezra's day. The guilty Israelites had entered unions that were illegal from the start because they were forbidden to Old Testament Jews by God's command (Deuteronomy 7:3). Malachi chapter 2 implies that many who had entered these intermarriages had broken marriages to Israelite wives in order to do so. The prophet Malachi speaks against "marrying the daughter of a foreign god" (verse 11) in the same context that he condemns divorcing "the wife of your youth" (verse 15). Malachi chapter 2 also strongly condemns the priests for their role in Israel's unfaithfulness.

Ezra's action of dissolving these mixed marriages was more comparable to telling someone to stop living in an adulterous relationship that was wrong from the start than to forcing someone to dissolve a valid marriage. Ezra required that the people obey the commandment that God had given them for the preservation of Israel, even though this undoubtedly caused pain and hardship for some of the wives who were sent away. The blame for the tragic side effects of this action belongs to those who had created the situation by ignoring God's law.

Today as well, people who ignore God's standards for faithfulness in marriage often cause pain to their spouses and innocent children. The responsibility for such an unhappy situation rests with those who created the problem by despising God's law. Ezra's harsh remedy was not without pain, but it prevented the greater evil of having Israel swallowed up by the surrounding peoples. A great threat to the restoration of the nation had been averted.

The list of the guilty

18Among the descendants of the priests, the following had married foreign women:

From the descendants of Jeshua son of Jozadak, and his brothers: Maaseiah, Eliezer, Jarib and Gedaliah. 19(They all gave their hands in pledge to put away their wives, and for their guilt they each presented a ram from the flock as a guilt offering.)
20From the descendants of Immer:
Hanani and Zebadiah.
21From the descendants of Harim:
Maaseiah, Elijah, Shemaiah, Jehiel and Uzziah.
22From the descendants of Pashhur:
Elioenai, Maaseiah, Ishmael, Nethanel, Jozabad and Elasah.

23Among the Levites:
Jozabad, Shimei, Kelaiah (that is, Kelita), Pethahiah, Judah and Eliezer.
24From the singers:
Eliashib.
From the gatekeepers:
Shallum, Telem and Uri.

25And among the other Israelites:
From the descendants of Parosh:
Ramiah, Izziah, Malkijah, Mijamin, Eleazar, Malkijah and Benaiah.

²⁶From the descendants of Elam:
Mattaniah, Zechariah, Jehiel, Abdi, Jeremoth and Elijah.
²⁷From the descendants of Zattu:
Elioenai, Eliashib, Mattaniah, Jeremoth, Zabad and Aziza.
²⁸From the descendants of Bebai:
Jehohanan, Hananiah, Zabbai and Athlai.
²⁹From the descendants of Bani:
Meshullam, Malluch, Adaiah, Jashub, Sheal and Jeremoth.
³⁰From the descendants of Pahath-Moab:
Adna, Kelal, Benaiah, Maaseiah, Mattaniah, Bezalel, Binnui
and Manasseh.
³¹From the descendants of Harim:
Eliezer, Ishijah, Malkijah, Shemaiah, Shimeon, ³²Benjamin,
Malluch and Shemariah.
³³From the descendants of Hashum:
Mattenai, Mattattah, Zabad, Eliphelet, Jeremai, Manasseh
and Shimei.
³⁴From the descendants of Bani:
Maadai, Amram, Uel, ³⁵Benaiah, Bedeiah, Keluhi,
³⁶Vaniah, Meremoth, Eliashib, ³⁷Mattaniah, Mattenai and
Jaasu.
³⁸From the descendants of Binnui:
Shimei, ³⁹Shelemiah, Nathan, Adaiah, ⁴⁰Macnadebai,
Shashai, Sharai, ⁴¹Azarel, Shelemiah, Shemariah, ⁴²Shallum,
Amariah and Joseph.
⁴³From the descendants of Nebo:
Jeiel, Mattithiah, Zabad, Zebina, Jaddai, Joel and Benaiah

⁴⁴All these had married foreign women, and some of them had
children by these wives.

The exact purpose of this list is not made clear in the
text. It does not seem likely that Ezra was trying to embar-
rass those listed; they had repented and had corrected the
situation.

The list is most likely intended to emphasize the seriousness of the sin. There are over one hundred names in the
list, and they may have been only the leaders. All of the
priestly families had become involved, even the descendants

of Jeshua son of Jozadak, the high priest who had led the restoration of the temple. The corruption had reached to the very heart of the nation and threatened its very existence. But the threat was averted, at least for the moment.

To us the list forms a rather abrupt finish to the book of Ezra. It seems to leave the story hanging in midair. This is appropriate because the story is not finished. The same problems and threats to Israel's existence that surfaced at the time of Ezra return in the book of Nehemiah. Our study of Nehemiah will really be another chapter of the same story we began in Ezra.

Nevertheless, the book of Ezra has led us through some important milestones in the history of Israel. A remnant of the nation has been reestablished in Judah and Jerusalem. The temple has been rebuilt, and worship there has been restored. The nation has survived serious threats to its existence. All these events testify to the grace of God in preserving Israel so that the promise of the Savior could be fulfilled. In the book of Nehemiah we will see how that grace continued.

INTRODUCTION TO NEHEMIAH

Background

The book of Nehemiah needs relatively little introduction. It continues the story begun in Ezra; most of the same circumstances and themes appearing in Ezra reoccur in Nehemiah. The two books are so closely connected that the Jewish rabbis and some versions of the Bible have treated them as one book. The book of Nehemiah has sometimes been called 2 Ezra.

There is, however, a valid basis for distinguishing the books as we do. Part of the book of Ezra refers to Ezra in the first person, indicating that he is the probable author of that book.

Much of the book of Nehemiah refers to Nehemiah in the first person, indicating that he is the apparent author of this book. All the action in this book centers on Nehemiah, except in chapters 8 and 9, where Ezra again appears to lead the reformation of Israel. Perhaps it was Ezra who took the memoirs of Nehemiah and added them to his own writings when the books of the Old Testament were collected.

The action described in the book of Nehemiah begins in the 20th year of King Artaxerxes of Persia (445 B.C.), about 12 years after the reformation led by Ezra. The spiritual condition of Judah had declined during this short period. Perhaps Ezra had returned to Persia to report to the king or to resume duties he had in Persia. He may have been away from Jerusalem for a number of years. Perhaps the lobbying against Jerusalem that is recorded in Ezra chapter 4 took place during Ezra's absence, although it seems more likely that it preceded the reforms of Ezra. At any rate, Nehemiah had to begin the restoration of Israel almost from scratch.

Outline

The book of Nehemiah records this rebuilding in two main parts. Chapters 1 to 7 report the restoration of the physical security of Jerusalem through the rebuilding of the city walls. Chapters 8 to 13 report the restoration of the spiritual security of Israel through the reforms carried out by Ezra and Nehemiah. The following outline will help you follow the line of thought of the book of Nehemiah as we progress with our study.

    I. Rebuilding the physical walls of Jerusalem
       (1:1–7:73)
       A. Nehemiah's prayer for Jerusalem (1:1-11)
       B. Nehemiah is sent to Jerusalem (2:1-10)
       C. Nehemiah prepares to rebuild the walls (2:11-20)
       D. The builders and their work (3:1-32)
       E. Opposition to the work (4:1–6:14)
       F. The wall completed despite opposition (6:15–7:3)
       G. The list of exiles who returned (7:4-73)

   II. Rebuilding the spiritual walls of Jerusalem (8:1–13:31)
       A. Ezra reads the law (8:1-12)
       B. The people celebrate (8:13-18)
       C. The Israelites make a covenant with the Lord
         (9:1–10:39)
       D. The Holy City is repopulated (11:1-36)
       E. The Levites' role in rebuilding Jerusalem (12:1-47)
       F. Nehemiah's final reforms (13:1-31)

PART ONE

Rebuilding the Physical Walls of Jerusalem
(1:1–7:73)

Nehemiah's prayer for Jerusalem

Nehemiah hears the plight of Jerusalem

1 **The words of Nehemiah son of Hacaliah:**
In the month of Kislev in the twentieth year, while I was in the citadel of Susa, ²Hanani, one of my brothers, came from Judah with some other men, and I questioned them about the Jewish remnant that survived the exile, and also about Jerusalem.

³They said to me, "Those who survived the exile and are back in the province are in great trouble and disgrace. The wall of Jerusalem is broken down, and its gates have been burned with fire."

⁴When I heard these things, I sat down and wept. For some days I mourned and fasted and prayed before the God of heaven.

Nehemiah was a high-ranking official in the Persian government. He was the king's cupbearer (1:11). As such, he was not a mere household servant but rather had a status equal to that of a member of the presidential cabinet in our government. Presenting the king's cup and protecting him against poisoning were a ceremonial part of Nehemiah's job, but he was also a trusted and influential advisor to the king. At the beginning of the book of Nehemiah, he was on duty in Susa, one of the Persian capital cities, located in what is now southern Iran. He received some visitors from faraway Jerusalem. These men may have been an official delegation from

Jerusalem, or they may have come for family or business purposes. If the words "one of my brothers" mean that Hanani was a real brother of Nehemiah, rather than simply a fellow Jew, it is more likely that this was not an official delegation.

It seems that Nehemiah learned of conditions in Jerusalem simply by making a casual inquiry. He was shocked to hear of the appalling situation there. Apparently, he had assumed that everything was fine since the mission of Ezra, about 12 years earlier. He had underestimated the persistence of Israel's enemies and the continued physical and spiritual weakness of the returnees. Nearly one hundred years after the return under Zerubbabel, Jerusalem still was not a secure city. Either the walls had never been rebuilt at all, or whatever work had been done had been undone by Israel's enemies. Even the restored temple, so vital to the nation, was exposed and was easy prey for enemies. The people were demoralized.

Nehemiah was grief stricken by what he heard. But he didn't despair. Instead, he gave evidence of his character as he turned to the only reliable source of help, the Lord his God.

Nehemiah's prayer

⁵**Then I said:**

> **"O LORD, God of heaven, the great and awesome God, who keeps his covenant of love with those who love him and obey his commands, ⁶let your ear be attentive and your eyes open to hear the prayer your servant is praying before you day and night for your servants, the people of Israel. I confess the sins we Israelites, including myself and my father's house, have committed against you. ⁷We have acted very wickedly toward you. We have not obeyed the commands, decrees and laws you gave your servant Moses.**
>
> ⁸**"Remember the instruction you gave your servant Moses, saying, 'If you are unfaithful, I will scatter you**

among the nations, ⁹but if you return to me and obey my commands, then even if your exiled people are at the farthest horizon, I will gather them from there and bring them to the place I have chosen as a dwelling for my Name.'

¹⁰"They are your servants and your people, whom you redeemed by your great strength and your mighty hand. ¹¹O Lord, let your ear be attentive to the prayer of this your servant and to the prayer of your servants who delight in revering your name. Give your servant success today by granting him favor in the presence of this man."

I was cupbearer to the king.

This prayer reveals much about Nehemiah. He felt the same oneness with God's people that Moses, Ezra, and other leaders of Israel had shown in the past. He was moved to intercede with the Lord on their behalf. Nehemiah had the same consciousness of sin that appeared in Ezra. He acknowledged his own sins and the sins of the people, but trusted the Lord for forgiveness. When any part of the body of Israel suffered, Nehemiah felt the pain. Nehemiah felt the same love and longing for Jerusalem that is expressed in so many of the psalms, notably Psalm 137. This devotion was especially remarkable since Nehemiah lived a thousand miles from Jerusalem—"the place . . . chosen as a dwelling for [God's] Name"—and had probably never been there.

Nehemiah's deep feelings, which may be hard for us to understand, were based on the fact that God had chosen a specific people, a specific land, and a special city as the scene of his actions to provide salvation for the whole world. There was only one chosen people from whom the Savior could be born as the seed of Abraham and David, namely, Israel. Jesus himself referred to this when he said, "Salvation is from the Jews" (John 4:22). There was only one Promised Land—God's plan had to be fulfilled in

Nehemiah, the king's cupbearer

Bethlehem and Jerusalem as the prophets had foretold (Micah 5:2; Zechariah 9:9). There was only one city— Jerusalem—where the sacrifices that pointed to the coming Savior could be offered. Nehemiah's love for the Lord and his hope of salvation could not be separated from his loyalty and love for the people, the land, and the city that God had chosen.

Today the true worship of God is no longer limited to one people or to any special place. "A time is coming," predicted Jesus, "when you will worship the Father neither on this mountain nor in Jerusalem . . . when the true worshipers will worship the Father in spirit and truth" (John 4:21,23). There still is a special people of God, the church of all believers. This church is sometimes called God's Israel, his new Jerusalem. We should feel the same bonds of love for God's people today, as Nehemiah did in his day. We can no more separate our love for God from love for his people than Nehemiah could. After all, "since God so loved us, we also ought to love one another" (1 John 4:11).

Nehemiah's prayer also reveals that he was a student of Scripture. The language of his prayer reflects the history of Israel and the promises of God as they were revealed in Scripture. The exodus, when God redeemed Israel from Egypt with his mighty hand and made them his chosen people, was the basis for Nehemiah's hope in the present difficulties. The middle part of his prayer echoed the warnings and promises recorded in Deuteronomy. The book of Deuteronomy must have been especially meaningful to believers in the days of Ezra and Nehemiah because it not only threatened the exile but also promised the return that they were experiencing. For example, Deuteronomy 30:4 states, "Even if you have been banished to the most distant land under the heavens, from there the LORD your God will gather you and bring you back."

In his prayer Nehemiah showed that although he was a servant of the king of Persia, he was first of all a servant of God. The king of Persia was a powerful world ruler, but in this matter he was no more than "this man." For all his power, he was still a man, not a god. Like everything else in this universe, he was subject to the God of heaven and earth. Nehemiah put his trust not in men but in the one true God, who always cares for his people.

If this prayer tells us a lot about Nehemiah, it also reveals a lot about God. He is the God of power, who rules and controls everything. The God of heaven, who rules the stars and planets, would have no trouble controlling a puny king, whose vast empire is like a drop in the bucket compared to the vastness of the universe. The Lord is great and awesome in his power. He is also awesome in his holiness. The threats of his law are not to be trifled with or despised. Israel had ignored the warnings given through Moses and had suffered the threatened devastation and exile. Now the nation was again flirting with disaster. The people needed to take warning from the way in which God had fulfilled his threats in the past, lest they provoke the awesome God by continued sin and impenitence.

In the 2,500 years that have passed since Nehemiah's time, God has not changed. Nor will he ever. He is still holy and awesome. He still threatens those who despise his Word. "It is a dreadful thing to fall into the hands of the living God" (Hebrews 10:31), "for our 'God is a consuming fire'" (Hebrews 12:29). We need to take warning so we don't repeat Israel's ingratitude and disobedience. But, above all, we need to remember that God is faithful to his covenant of love. He has made a covenant—that is, a promise, a commitment—to forgive our sins. "This is the covenant I will make with the house of Israel. . . . I will forgive their wickedness and will remember their sins no more" (Jeremiah 31:33,34). God will never break that promise; it rests on his own truthfulness and on the completed work of Christ. When in weakness we sin, we can confess our sins as Nehemiah did. And we can enjoy the same confidence of forgiveness he had. This is possible because our confidence does not depend on our own achievements but on the promises of God.

Nehemiah is sent to Jerusalem

2 **In the month of Nisan in the twentieth year of King Artaxerxes, when wine was brought for him, I took the wine and gave it to the king. I had not been sad in his presence before; ²so the king asked me, "Why does your face look so sad when you are not ill? This can be nothing but sadness of heart."**

I was very much afraid, ³but I said to the king, "May the king live forever! Why should my face not look sad when the city where my fathers are buried lies in ruins, and its gates have been destroyed by fire?"

⁴The king said to me, "What is it you want?"

Then I prayed to the God of heaven, ⁵and I answered the king, "If it pleases the king and if your servant has found favor in his sight, let him send me to the city in Judah where my fathers are buried so that I can rebuild it."

⁶Then the king, with the queen sitting beside him, asked me, "How long will your journey take, and when will you get back?" It pleased the king to send me; so I set a time.

⁷I also said to him, "If it pleases the king, may I have letters to the governors of Trans-Euphrates, so that they will provide me safe-conduct until I arrive in Judah? ⁸And may I have a letter to Asaph, keeper of the king's forest, so he will give me timber to make beams for the gates of the citadel by the temple and for the city wall and for the residence I will occupy?" And because the gracious hand of my God was upon me, the king granted my

requests. ⁹**So I went to the governors of Trans-Euphrates and gave them the king's letters. The king had also sent army officers and cavalry with me.**
¹⁰**When Sanballat the Horonite and Tobiah the Ammonite official heard about this, they were very much disturbed that someone had come to promote the welfare of the Israelites.**

Three months passed between the time when Nehemiah had heard of the plight of Jerusalem and when he asked the king for help. We do not know if fear held Nehemiah back or if he simply didn't have a good opportunity to make his plea. Nehemiah finally presented his case when the king inquired about his sad appearance. Nehemiah's fear may have been due to the fact that sadness was considered inappropriate in the presence of the great king. Furthermore, if his request were rejected, he could lose his status, his job, or perhaps even his life.

In that moment while his heart was pounding with fear, Nehemiah directed a brief, silent prayer to the Lord. This was very typical of Nehemiah, who is shown as a man of prayer throughout this book. Nehemiah's prayer demonstrates the meaning of the scriptural admonition "Pray continually" (1 Thessalonians 5:17). Nehemiah had no time for lengthy or formal prayer, but he showed that continual prayer is basically an attitude of the heart. It is trusting in God at all times and facing each new situation with an awareness of our dependence on God's help. Nehemiah faced his crisis with an unspoken plea for help. Emboldened by his confidence that the Lord would answer his prayer, Nehemiah pursued his case.

Nehemiah's request indicated that he already had a well-formed plan in mind. He knew which officials he needed to contact for lumber from the royal forests and which he needed to contact to receive adequate protection for his activities. Unlike Ezra, Nehemiah was not hesitant to make use of whatever military escort the king might provide. It seems that Nehemiah realized he would not be able to cope with officials who opposed his plans unless he himself received the status of a self-sufficient governor. Nehemiah's plans were well laid, but when he succeeded, he attributed his success to the hand of God, which was upon him.

As for King Artaxerxes, his readiness to grant Nehemiah's request was based on more than just being bighearted. The rich province of Egypt was restless. It was in Persia's best interest to have the Palestinian province in friendly, loyal hands. Assisting the Jews in rebuilding their ruined capital would help ensure that.

As he began his mission, Nehemiah combined trust in God with a determination to use all the resources with which he had been blessed. From the start he realized that he faced a real battle and would need all the strength available to him in order to triumph.

Opposition to Nehemiah's plans appears to have solidified before he reached Jerusalem and even before the exact nature of his plans was clear. Sanballat the Horonite was probably the governor of Samaria. The meaning of the term *Horonite* is uncertain. It may indicate that Sanballat was from the town of Beth Horon, northwest of Jerusalem. If Judah had been part of one province with Samaria before Nehemiah's arrival, Sanballat's opposition may have been partly due to fear that Nehemiah was receiving some of his territory.

Ammon was a region east of the Jordan River and had long been Israel's rival. Non-biblical records show that this area was ruled by a Tobiad family not long after this time. The Tobiah in our text seems to be one of the first of this line. His exact position is uncertain. The word translated "official" is literally "slave," or "servant." He may have been a Persian appointee who was under the supervision of Sanballat. At any rate, the most powerful political figures in the area were set against Nehemiah's plans from the start. Nehemiah had his work cut out for him.

Nehemiah prepares to rebuild the walls

¹¹I went to Jerusalem, and after staying there three days ¹²I set out during the night with a few men. I had not told anyone what my God had put in my heart to do for Jerusalem. There were no mounts with me except the one I was riding on.

¹³By night I went out through the Valley Gate toward the Jackal Well and the Dung Gate, examining the walls of Jerusalem, which had been broken down, and its gates, which had been destroyed by fire. ¹⁴Then I moved on toward the Fountain Gate and the King's Pool, but there was not enough room for my mount to get through; ¹⁵so I went up the valley by night, examining the wall. Finally, I turned back and reentered through the Valley Gate. ¹⁶The officials did not know where I had gone or what I was doing, because as yet I had said nothing to the Jews or the priests or nobles or officials or any others who would be doing the work.

¹⁷Then I said to them, "You see the trouble we are in: Jerusalem lies in ruins, and its gates have been burned with fire. Come, let us rebuild the wall of Jerusalem, and we will no longer be in disgrace." ¹⁸I also told them about the gracious hand of my God upon me and what the king had said to me.

They replied, "Let us start rebuilding." So they began this good work.

¹⁹But when Sanballat the Horonite, and Tobiah the Ammonite official and Geshem the Arab heard about it, they mocked and ridiculed us. "What is this you are doing?" they asked. "Are you rebelling against the king?"

²⁰I answered them by saying, "The God of heaven will give us success. We his servants will start rebuilding, but as for you, you have no share in Jerusalem or any claim or historic right to it."

Nehemiah tried to keep his plan as secret as possible. No doubt Sanballat and Tobiah had informants in Jerusalem who would report every move Nehemiah made. The goal of Nehemiah's night inspection of the ruins was to organize the work so that it could be completed as quickly as possible after it was begun. In this way Sanballat and Tobiah would have little opportunity to organize their opposition.

Nehemiah soon won the support of Jerusalem's leaders when he presented his credentials and his plan. He persuaded them that he not only had authority from the Persian king, but, more important, he had the blessing of God on his project. The restoration of Jerusalem's walls would remove the disgrace and sad reminder of its destruction and would provide security for the returnees. The people were eager to begin the work: "Let us start rebuilding."

As soon as the rebuilding began, however, Sanballat and Tobiah started their campaign to intimidate the builders. They were joined in this by Geshem the Arab. Like Sanballat and Tobiah, Geshem is mentioned in other surviving historical texts from this period. They refer to him as the ruler of Kedar. These three men are examples of historical characters in the Bible whose existences have recently been confirmed by other sources. While such outside sources do not "prove" the Bible is true, they bear witness that Scripture's history is reliable and accurate. This is just what we can expect from God, whose "word is truth" (John 17:17).

The enemies' attempt at intimidation was based on a two-pronged attack. First, they hoped that their ridicule of the Jews' weakness would cause the Jews to despair of their ability to complete the project and give up before they even began. If this failed, the enemies hoped to plant doubts about Nehemiah's intentions. If he was building the walls as the first step in a revolt against Persia, Nehemiah could well bring destruction on Israel, just as other leaders of Israel had done by revolting against Assyria and Babylon.

Nehemiah had an apt reply to both tactics. The Jews would succeed in spite of their weakness, because God would bless their efforts. They were not building the city to rebel against Persia but to honor God. Furthermore, Nehemiah reminded Sanballat and his allies that they would do well to mind their own business. They had no religious rights in Jerusalem, because they did not follow the true worship of the Lord. Nor did they have any political rights in Jerusalem, because the Persian king had assigned that authority to Nehemiah, not to them. After rejecting their taunts, Nehemiah and his followers were determined to get on with the work of rebuilding.

It is difficult to understand the descriptions of the rebuilding of Jerusalem in this and following chapters without some description of the terrain of Old Testament Jerusalem. The identification of some of the places mentioned is uncertain, but the map entitled "Nehemiah's Jerusalem," page 201, shows the most likely locations and will help you follow the descriptions in the text.

Ancient Jerusalem stood on three large hills. The smallest of these hills, Ophel, made up the southeast quarter of the city. This was the original city of David. Mount Moriah, where Solomon built the temple, formed the northeastern part of the city. After the time of Solomon the city spread westward onto the largest hill, which is now called Mount Zion.

Deep valleys surrounded the whole city. The Tyropoean Valley, separating Ophel from Mount Zion, divided Jerusalem down the middle.

It is likely that Nehemiah's Jerusalem did not cover the entire area the city had occupied before its destruction. Rather, it was limited to Ophel and part of the temple

Nehemiah inspecting Jerusalem's walls

mountain. Jerusalem had become a small city, covering only about 30 acres with room for about 5,000 inhabitants.

As the map indicates, the Valley Gate, where Nehemiah began his inspection, is on the west side of Ophel. He traveled down the Tyropoean Valley to the Dung Gate and Jackal Well at the southern tip of the city. The Jackal or Serpent Well may be the spring En Rogel mentioned elsewhere in the Old Testament. For example, centuries before Nehemiah's time, back in the days of Joshua, En Rogel was on the border between the tribes of Benjamin and Judah (Joshua 15:7; 18:16). The Fountain Gate and King's Pool appear to be designations for the area around the pool that the New Testament calls the Pool of Siloam. At this place Jesus healed a blind man (John 9:1-11). The massive amount of rubble strewn down the slopes when the city was destroyed made Nehemiah's night inspection extremely difficult. Finally he was able to make his way back to his starting point. It is not certain from the text whether he succeeded in getting all the way around the city or was forced to retrace his steps after getting only partway around. The latter seems more likely.

This section emphasizes the difficulties Nehemiah faced. Strong enemies threatened danger from without. The great devastation made the task of rebuilding immense. But with the help of God, Nehemiah completed the preparations for a successful project.

The builders and their work

Chapter 3 contains another long list of names like the lists that occur so often in Ezra and Nehemiah. Because the places and people named are strange to us, we might find it difficult to get much out of reading these lists. But, like all of Scripture, these lists have a practical value.

The mention of each person who led the building of a portion of the wall reminds us that no work of love performed for the Lord ever goes unnoticed or forgotten. The stories of the widow's mite (Luke 21:1-4) and Mary's anointing of Jesus (John 12:1-8) are other portions of Scripture we might call stewardship memorials. These passages provide examples of stewardship and assure us that God will record and remember our deeds of love, even though others may not notice or remember them. Anyone who gives even "a cup of cold water" in Christ's name "will certainly not lose his reward" (Matthew 10:42). Reading chapter 3 will be more meaningful if we remember that each unfamiliar name is a memorial to some deed of love. We will thank God for the way in which he creates willing hearts in believers of all generations.

This list also demonstrates Nehemiah's careful preparation and organization. Each leader had his own area and responsibilities clearly outlined. The work was organized so that the whole wall could be rebuilt simultaneously. Nehemiah chose this method so the work could be completed in the shortest time possible, in order to frustrate Sanballat's attempts to interfere.

Nehemiah chapter 3 provides one of the most comprehensive descriptions of Old Testament Jerusalem. Consequently, it is valuable for students of biblical geography and history.

The northern wall

3 **Eliashib the high priest and his fellow priests went to work and rebuilt the Sheep Gate. They dedicated it and set its doors in place, building as far as the Tower of the Hundred, which they dedicated, and as far as the Tower of Hananel. ²The men of Jericho built the adjoining section, and Zaccur son of Imri built next to them.**

³**The Fish Gate was rebuilt by the sons of Hassenaah. They laid its beams and put its doors and bolts and bars in place. ⁴Meremoth son of Uriah, the son of Hakkoz, repaired the next section. Next to him Meshullam son of Berekiah, the son of Meshezabel, made repairs, and next to him Zadok son of Baana also made repairs. ⁵The next section was repaired by the men of Tekoa, but their nobles would not put their shoulders to the work under their supervisors.**

Nehemiah begins his description of Jerusalem at the northeast corner of the city, probably so that the high priest and his crew could be placed in the position of honor. The northern wall was the most important and required the heaviest fortifications, since the city had the poorest natural defenses in this direction. The city gates were not simply doors in the walls, but strong, roofed towers that contained a number of guardhouses inside. The gates were one of the most vital parts of the fortifications.

Some workers from nearby villages joined the priests in rebuilding the northern wall. The only sour note was the lack of cooperation by the nobles from Tekoa. The prophet Amos had lived near this town about a dozen miles south of Jerusalem (Amos 1:1).

The western wall

⁶**The Jeshanah Gate was repaired by Joiada son of Paseah and Meshullam son of Besodeiah. They laid its beams and put its doors and bolts and bars in place. ⁷Next to them, repairs were made by men from Gibeon and Mizpah—Melatiah of Gibeon and Jadon of Meronoth—places under the authority of the governor of Trans-Euphrates. ⁸Uzziel son of Harhaiah, one of the goldsmiths, repaired the next section; and Hananiah, one of the perfume-makers, made repairs next to that. They restored Jerusalem as far as the Broad Wall. ⁹Rephaiah son of Hur, ruler of a half-district of Jerusalem, repaired the next section. ¹⁰Adjoining this, Jedaiah son**

of Harumaph made repairs opposite his house, and Hattush son of Hashabneiah made repairs next to him. ¹¹Malkijah son of Harim and Hasshub son of Pahath-Moab repaired another section and the Tower of the Ovens. ¹²Shallum son of Hallohesh, ruler of a half-district of Jerusalem, repaired the next section with the help of his daughters.

When people are named as the restorers of a section of the western wall, this probably means they donated money to pay for the specified section, rather than implies that they did all the work themselves. These people were probably leading citizens of their areas. Gibeon and Mizpah were north of Jerusalem in territory that was apparently not under Nehemiah's jurisdiction, but under the control of another Persian governor, perhaps Sanballat. If this was the case, these people were taking a special risk by participating. The references to the goldsmiths, perfumers, and to other crafts-men, here and in other sections of the chapter, imply that craftsmen in Israel may have been organized into guilds or associations of some sort.

We have little information about the specific fortifica-tions named in this section. The Broad Wall may be the wall encircling the western hill called Mount Zion. Nehemiah's refortification program ended at this wall. The work included only the inner walls around the temple mount and Ophel.

The southwestern wall

¹³The Valley Gate was repaired by Hanun and the residents of Zanoah. They rebuilt it and put its doors and bolts and bars in place. They also repaired five hundred yards of the wall as far as the Dung Gate.

¹⁴The Dung Gate was repaired by Malkijah son of Recab, ruler of the district of Beth Hakkerem. He rebuilt it and put its doors and bolts and bars in place.

These verses describe the wall that ran along the western edge of Ophel. The Valley Gate, the gate used by Nehemiah on his inspection trip, opened out onto the Tyropoean Valley, the valley that divided Ophel from Mount Zion. The Dung Gate was at the southern tip of the city. Its name implies that it was through the Dung Gate that garbage was carried to the dump outside the city.

The eastern wall

[15]The Fountain Gate was repaired by Shallun son of Col-Hozeh, ruler of the district of Mizpah. He rebuilt it, roofing it over and putting its doors and bolts and bars in place. He also repaired the wall of the Pool of Siloam, by the King's Garden, as far as the steps going down from the City of David. [16]Beyond him, Nehemiah son of Azbuk, ruler of a half-district of Beth Zur, made repairs up to a point opposite the tombs of David, as far as the artificial pool and the House of the Heroes.

[17]Next to him, the repairs were made by the Levites under Rehum son of Bani. Beside him, Hashabiah, ruler of half the district of Keilah, carried out repairs for his district. [18]Next to him, the repairs were made by their countrymen under Binnui son of Henadad, ruler of the other half-district of Keilah. [19]Next to him, Ezer son of Jeshua, ruler of Mizpah, repaired another section, from a point facing the ascent to the armory as far as the angle. [20]Next to him, Baruch son of Zabbai zealously repaired another section, from the angle to the entrance of the house of Eliashib the high priest. [21]Next to him, Meremoth son of Uriah, the son of Hakkoz, repaired another section, from the entrance of Eliashib's house to the end of it.

[22]The repairs next to him were made by the priests from the surrounding region. [23]Beyond them, Benjamin and Hasshub made repairs in front of their house; and next to them, Azariah son of Maaseiah, the son of Ananiah, made repairs beside his house. [24]Next to him, Binnui son of Henadad, repaired another section, from Azariah's house to the angle and the corner, [25]and Palal son of Uzai worked opposite the angle and the tower projecting from

the upper palace near the court of the guard. Next to him, Pedaiah son of Parosh ²⁶and the temple servants living on the hill of Ophel made repairs up to a point opposite the Water Gate toward the east and the projecting tower. ²⁷Next to them, the men of Tekoa repaired another section, from the great projecting tower to the wall of Ophel.

²⁸Above the Horse Gate, the priests made repairs, each in front of his own house. ²⁹Next to them, Zadok son of Immer made repairs opposite his house. Next to him, Shemaiah son of Shecaniah, the guard at the East Gate, made repairs. ³⁰Next to him, Hananiah son of Shelemiah, and Hanun, the sixth son of Zalaph, repaired another section. Next to them, Meshullam son of Berekiah made repairs opposite his living quarters. ³¹Next to him, Malkijah, one of the goldsmiths, made repairs as far as the house of the temple servants and the merchants, opposite the Inspection Gate, and as far as the room above the corner; ³²and between the room above the corner and the Sheep Gate the goldsmiths and merchants made repairs.

These verses describe the wall that ran along the eastern side of Ophel and the temple mount, overlooking the Kidron Valley. The exact nature and location of many features of this section of the wall are uncertain, but we can describe a few of the main features.

The Pool of Siloam was a large reservoir of water brought from a nearby spring by tunnel and aqueduct. Its basic outline is still visible today. The nearby "artificial pool" may be the same as the King's Pool mentioned in Nehemiah chapter 2. The exact relationship of the various storage pools in this area to those that still exist today is uncertain. The Fountain Gate apparently gave access to one of Jerusalem's two main springs, the spring En Rogel, which was southeast of the city walls in the Kidron Valley. The Water Gate was the main gate in the middle of the eastern wall of the City of David. It led to the spring Gihon, the most important water source for Old Testament Jerusalem and the source of the water that was stored in Siloam and the other pools.

All these details stress the importance of water sources for an ancient city. Water sources were especially critical for a city like Jerusalem, where there is no rain for five or six months each summer. Water was collected in reservoirs and cisterns during the rainy season, so that women could go to these places to draw water during the dry season.

The royal tombs of David and his dynasty, or descendants, were apparently located on the southeastern slopes of Ophel. The nearby House of Heroes may have been a memorial to David's mighty men. The location of the various corners and towers in the eastern wall is uncertain. The northeastern section of Ophel is the only place where archaeologists have to date discovered the foundations of Nehemiah's wall. In this area Nehemiah's wall is located farther up the slope than the original wall of David's city. When the text refers to an individual working "opposite" some tower or landmark, it may be referring to a position farther up the slope across from the ruins of those earlier fortifications.

These questions are difficult to resolve, but none of them changes the meaning of the text for us. Studying a text like this gives us some idea of the difficulties that archaeologists, historians, and mapmakers face as they try to reconstruct Old Testament Jerusalem. Since extensive excavations are now being conducted on Ophel, some of these questions may be clarified in the near future.

The builders of this section of the wall were an interesting mix of people. Some lived next to the section of the wall they were building; others were from towns in Judah and had come to help rebuild the city that would be their spiritual and religious capital. This reminds us of how we build mission congregations today. The founding of such congregations is usually a joint effort of Christians who live in a community and those who live elsewhere. Those living in the immediate area of the mission church will benefit directly from its services. The others lend their support of prayers and gifts from a distance. They want to help the new congregation get on its feet because they believe in its work. The rebuilding of Jerusalem's walls was a good example of the cooperation of believers from different places. They worked together on a project that would be a blessing to all of them.

Opposition to the work

The enemy scoffs; God's people pray

4 **When Sanballat heard that we were rebuilding the wall, he became angry and was greatly incensed. He ridiculed the Jews, ²and in the presence of his associates and the army of Samaria, he said, "What are those feeble Jews doing? Will they restore their wall? Will they offer sacrifices? Will they finish in a day? Can they bring the stones back to life from those heaps of rubble—burned as they are?"**

³Tobiah the Ammonite, who was at his side, said, "What they are building—if even a fox climbed up on it, he would break down their wall of stones!"

⁴Hear us, O our God, for we are despised. Turn their insults back on their own heads. Give them over as plunder in a land of captivity. ⁵Do not cover up their guilt or blot out their sins from your sight, for they have thrown insults in the face of the builders.

⁶So we rebuilt the wall till all of it reached half its height, for the people worked with all their heart.

Because of Nehemiah's organization and the people's eagerness, the work of rebuilding Jerusalem's wall progressed rapidly. But wherever God's work is being done, Satan works overtime to create opposition.

Sanballat, the ringleader of Israel's enemies, was enraged to hear that the rebuilding project was making rapid progress despite his recent attempts to discourage the work. He angrily stepped up his campaign of intimidation. He publicly heaped scorn on the "feeble Jews" and their efforts to restore Jerusalem. Playing the role of Sanballat's stooge, Tobiah sarcastically derided the Jews' effort. City walls were supposed to be able to withstand the pounding of heavy siege machinery, he scoffed, but the Jews' puny efforts wouldn't even stand up under the weight of a little fox! With their scorn and sarcasm, Sanballat and Tobiah hoped to strengthen the confidence of God's enemies and discourage God's people.

Such scorn was nothing new, and it is still around today. Throughout history unbelievers have scoffed at the humble means God uses to fulfill his promises. It was that way in Abraham's family. Ishmael scoffed at little Isaac as the bearer of the promise (Genesis 21:8-14). Goliath cursed David and the God in whose name David came (1 Samuel 17). Christ himself endured scorn throughout his life because he came in lowliness. Today the unbelieving world still heaps scorn on God's Word and the quiet way it works. Many demand that the church perform the task of reforming society; they deride the fact that the church cannot even eliminate sin in the lives of its own members, much less in society as a whole. But God's faithful servants ignore the scorn and stick to the job God has given them. In this way, God's work is done, the gospel continues its quiet march, and God's kingdom advances forcefully.

In one respect Sanballat and Tobiah were right. The builders of Jerusalem were feeble if they depended on their own power. They did not have great numbers. They did not have great wealth. All they had was faith and the promise of God that supported that faith. But it was all they needed. With God-given courage they continued to work and left the judging of their enemies to God.

Because he calls for judgment on his enemies, some have criticized Nehemiah's prayer as being unforgiving and unchristian. Isn't such a prayer contrary to the example of

Jesus on the cross, when he prayed for his enemies (Luke 23:34)? And doesn't the rest of the Bible teach us to forgive our enemies? For example, Jesus says, "Love your enemies" (Matthew 5:44), and Saint Paul declares: "Bless those who persecute you. . . . Do not repay anyone evil for evil. . . . Do not take revenge. . . . If your enemy is hungry, feed him" (Romans 12:14,17,19,20).

Yet the Bible also contains Nehemiah's seemingly vengeful prayer. Nor is it alone. Such prayers for judgment occur frequently in the Scriptures. Psalms 7; 35; 58; 59; 69:19-28; 109; 137:7-9; and 139:19-22 furnish examples of such prayers. These psalms are called imprecatory psalms, or cursing psalms.

Some commentators attempt to explain away these imprecatory passages by saying that believers in Old Testament times were at a lower level of religious advancement than we are today. According to this view, the coming of the New Testament has made such prayers obsolete. But such an explanation will not hold up. Psalm 69, one of the psalms that includes a curse, is a Messianic psalm, referring to Christ. The New Testament quotes it as such. John 15:25, for instance, takes the words of Psalm 69:4 and applies them to Christ: "They hated me without reason." In this psalm it is Christ, the Messiah, who asks God the Father to judge his enemies. The curses of Psalm 69:25 are quoted in Acts 1:20 as being fulfilled in the judgment against Judas: "It is written in the book of Psalms, 'May his place be deserted; let there be no one to dwell in it.'" Even the saints in heaven pray for God's avenging judgment to fall on the persecutors of the church: "How long, Sovereign Lord, holy and true, until you judge the inhabitants of the earth and avenge our blood?" (Revelation 6:10).

But how can such prayers be reconciled with the gospel proclamation that the Lord is a forgiving God? The God who promises forgiveness in the gospel is the same God who threatens in his law to punish all who despise him. Those who despise God's promise and work to oppose his plans remain under the wrath of God. God said that he would bless those who blessed Abraham, the bearer of the promise, and curse those who cursed Abraham (Genesis 12:3). This is simply another way of saying that God will bring deserved judgment on those who work for Satan, who try to destroy the line of the Savior and the children of God. We cannot wish such people success without setting ourselves against the will of God. David could not pray that the evil plans of Saul and Absalom would succeed, because if they did, God's promise would have failed. Nor could Nehemiah pray that Sanballat's plans to thwart the restoration of Israel would succeed. If they did, God's promises would not have been fulfilled.

Today we should pray that our enemies and God's enemies will come to repentance. But we must also pray that their attacks on God's kingdom come to nothing. Martin Luther once wrote, "We cannot pray the Lord's Prayer without cursing." Every time we pray, "Hallowed be your name, your kingdom come, your will be done," we are in a sense cursing. As Luther writes in his explanation of the Third Petition of the Lord's Prayer: "God's will is done when he breaks and defeats every evil plan and purpose of the devil, the world, and our sinful flesh, which try to prevent us from keeping God's name holy and letting his kingdom come."

Like David, Nehemiah did not attack his enemies or seek personal revenge. He left their judgment to God. Yet Nehemiah was right in praying that God would frustrate the enemies' efforts. Then, with faith in God's power and promises, he carried on his work. The scorn of God's enemies cannot stop those who trust in God.

The enemy threatens; God's people stand firm

⁷But when Sanballat, Tobiah, the Arabs, the Ammonites and the men of Ashdod heard that the repairs to Jerusalem's walls had gone ahead and that the gaps were being closed, they were very angry. ⁸They all plotted together to come and fight against Jerusalem and stir up trouble against it. ⁹But we prayed to our God and posted a guard day and night to meet this threat.

¹⁰Meanwhile, the people in Judah said, "The strength of the laborers is giving out, and there is so much rubble that we cannot rebuild the wall."

¹¹Also our enemies said, "Before they know it or see us, we will be right there among them and will kill them and put an end to the work."

¹²Then the Jews who lived near them came and told us ten times over, "Wherever you turn, they will attack us."

¹³Therefore I stationed some of the people behind the lowest points of the wall at the exposed places, posting them by families, with their swords, spears and bows. ¹⁴After I looked things over, I stood up and said to the nobles, the officials and the rest of the people, "Don't be afraid of them. Remember the Lord, who is great and awesome, and fight for your brothers, your sons and your daughters, your wives and your homes."

When bluster and big talk failed to stop the work on the walls, the enemies had to put up or shut up. To stop the building, they would have to attack Jerusalem. Now they couldn't just sit around and talk smart; they would have to risk their lives in battle.

Everything seemed to be in the enemies' favor. Judah was surrounded by enemies on all sides—the Samaritans on the north, the Ammonites across the Jordan to the east, the Arabs on the south, and now Ashdod, a city of the Philistines, joined the coalition on the west. With such a coalition, the enemies must have assumed that the attack on the unfinished walls would be easy. Even if the attack was not entirely successful, perhaps King Artaxerxes would have second thoughts about supporting any project that was going to cause disorder in the provinces. He might well decide to cancel the rebuilding of the walls.

Nehemiah thwarted the enemies' plans with a two-pronged defense. He entrusted Jerusalem's cause to the Lord in prayer, and he set up a strong military defense. These two measures were complementary, not contradictory. It is not a lack of trust in God to use all the means that he has put at our disposal. For example, in time of sickness, we should pray for the sick person, but we should also use medicine and the other natural means that God has given us. We will pray for the spread of the gospel, but we will also get out and eagerly share the gospel with others. The motto of the medieval monks—"work and pray"—is a good policy in any undertaking.

Nehemiah posted the people at their battle stations, ready to repel the expected attack. He aroused their courage by calling their attention to two reasons for boldness in battle. First and most important, they had the great and awesome God on their side, so they had nothing to fear. In addition, the lives of their families were at stake, so they should fight with all their strength. Thus prepared, the people stood firm and awaited the attack. But the enemies' mouths were bigger than their hearts. Their game was talking big and attacking defenseless cities, not throwing themselves against armed troops occupying fortified positions.

Nehemiah's prayer was answered. The attack never came because the enemies' courage failed them. The work could resume.

Threats can't stop the work

[15]When our enemies heard that we were aware of their plot and that God had frustrated it, we all returned to the wall, each to his own work.

¹⁶From that day on, half of my men did the work, while the other half were equipped with spears, shields, bows and armor. The officers posted themselves behind all the people of Judah ¹⁷who were building the wall. Those who carried materials did their work with one hand and held a weapon in the other, ¹⁸and each of the builders wore his sword at his side as he worked. But the man who sounded the trumpet stayed with me.

¹⁹Then I said to the nobles, the officials and the rest of the people, "The work is extensive and spread out, and we are widely separated from each other along the wall. ²⁰Wherever you hear the sound of the trumpet, join us there. Our God will fight for us!"

²¹So we continued the work with half the men holding spears, from the first light of dawn till the stars came out. ²²At that time I also said to the people, "Have every man and his helper stay inside Jerusalem at night, so they can serve as guards by night and workmen by day." ²³Neither I nor my brothers nor my men nor the guards with me took off our clothes; each had his weapon, even when he went for water.

After the enemies had revealed their cowardice and called off their attack, Nehemiah and his people could leave their battle stations and return to work. But because of the treachery of the enemy, they had to stay on permanent alert to guard against a sneak attack.

Nehemiah took a number of security precautions. Half the workforce was put on guard duty. Other workers carried weapons as they worked. A trumpeter was to sound the alarm in case there was an attack. Those who commuted to Jerusalem for the work were now to stay in the city to provide a greater force against night attacks. This would also cut down on traffic in and out of the city at dawn and dusk and so reduce the risk of infiltration. With these precautions, the Jews seemed to have beaten the enemies outside Jerusalem. Sad to say, the enemy within was just as dangerous.

Opposition from within

5 Now the men and their wives raised a great outcry against their Jewish brothers. [2]Some were saying, "We and our sons and daughters are numerous; in order for us to eat and stay alive, we must get grain."

[3]Others were saying, "We are mortgaging our fields, our vineyards and our homes to get grain during the famine."

[4]Still others were saying, "We have had to borrow money to pay the king's tax on our fields and vineyards. [5]Although we are of the same flesh and blood as our countrymen and though our sons are as good as theirs, yet we have to subject our sons and daughters to slavery. Some of our daughters have already been enslaved, but we are powerless, because our fields and our vineyards belong to others."

[6]When I heard their outcry and these charges, I was very angry. [7]I pondered them in my mind and then accused the nobles and officials. I told them, "You are exacting usury from your own countrymen!" So I called together a large meeting to deal with them [8]and said, "As far as possible, we have bought back our Jewish brothers who were sold to the Gentiles. Now you are selling your brothers, only for them to be sold back to us!" They kept quiet, because they could find nothing to say.

[9]So I continued, "What you are doing is not right. Shouldn't you walk in the fear of our God to avoid the reproach of our Gentile enemies? [10]I and my brothers and my men are also lending the people money and grain. But let the exacting of usury stop! [11]Give back to them immediately their fields, vineyards, olive groves and houses, and also the usury you are charging them—the hundredth part of the money, grain, new wine and oil."

[12]"We will give it back," they said. "And we will not demand anything more from them. We will do as you say."

Then I summoned the priests and made the nobles and officials take an oath to do what they had promised. [13]I also shook out the folds of my robe and said, "In this way may God shake out of his house and possessions every man who does not keep this promise. So may such a man be shaken out and emptied!"

At this the whole assembly said, "Amen," and praised the LORD. And the people did as they had promised.

"They are their own worst enemies." This cliché certainly applied to the Jews of Nehemiah's day. Just when it seemed they had beaten their enemies on the outside, dissension and division from within threatened the success of the rebuilding project. In our day too, when the church enjoys rest from its enemies and a period of peace to carry out its mission, Satan raises division and strife within the church to divert it from its work.

In Nehemiah's time Satan's method was leading the rich to exploit the poor. Famine, large families to feed, the heavy Persian taxes—all these factors combined to drive the poor Jewish farmers into bankruptcy. The farmers' willingness to help rebuild the walls of Jerusalem may even have contributed to their plight. The time they spent in Jerusalem and away from their farms could only have worsened their situation. Their undefended farms were undoubtedly open to raids by Sanballat's men. Seeing the rich take advantage of the poor made the poor people even more resentful of their economic position. When taking out mortgages on their land was not enough to pay their debts, they were forced into the desperate action of selling their children into slavery. It was either that or starvation for them and their children.

In ancient times people sometimes preferred slavery to a good master to freedom. The room and board a slave received offered relative security in comparison to the hand-to-mouth existence of the poor freeman. But slavery, though it offered some security, was still a humiliation for Israelites. God had redeemed them from their slavery in Egypt. Slavery could be especially humiliating for the daughters, since female slaves were sometimes used as secondary wives.

For these reasons the Lord had restricted the existence of slavery among the Israelites (Exodus 21:2-11; Leviticus 25:39-55; Deuteronomy 15:12-18). No Israelite could be held in slavery as a result of debt for more than six years. Then he had to be freed. A female slave who had been used as a wife could not be sold, but either had to keep her rights as a wife or go free. No family farm in Israel could be permanently sold but had to be returned to its original owner in the Year of Jubilee, that is, every 50th year. When Israelites were forced to borrow money from one another to obtain the necessities of life, they were not to be charged any interest. Israelites who had the means to help their less fortunate countrymen were to lend them what they needed to live, even when the lenders could expect no economic return from providing such help (Exodus 22:25-27; Leviticus 25:35-37; Deuteronomy 23:19,20). Helping a fellow member of God's chosen people was to be an act of charity, not a business proposition.

Nehemiah's contemporaries were flagrantly ignoring these provisions of God's law. It appears they were not only exacting interest from their distressed neighbors, but were also selling them into slavery to foreigners. They could get a better price by selling them to foreigners, because the six-year limit on servitude was not observed by non-Israelites. But then there was no way that the slaves could gain their freedom, unless another Israelite paid the price of their ransoms.

The interest in ancient times was often figured on a monthly basis, so the "hundredth part" probably refers to 12 percent per year. While this figure doesn't seem exorbitant in comparison with interest rates today, it was more than the poor could handle under the circumstances of Nehemiah's time. What made matters worse was that this sin of economic exploitation was one of the sins that had been responsible for the judgment of captivity that had befallen

Israel. The prophets Isaiah (5:8), Jeremiah (34:8-22), and Amos (2:6-8; 4:1; 5:11) had denounced this sin. Amos' words of warning were typical: "You trample on the poor and force him to give you grain. Therefore, though you have built stone mansions, you will not live in them; though you have planted lush vineyards, you will not drink their wine" (5:11). But these warnings had been ignored. Now the Jews were again drifting back into these same sins that had caused the captivity, just as they had in the case of intermarriage. Furthermore, this sin of economic exploitation was stripping the land of the workers whom God had restored to Israel, just when they were needed the most.

Nehemiah was outraged when he heard of this sin and immediately took measures to put an end to it. He strongly denounced the practice and exacted a promise that such exploitation would be stopped. He dramatized his condemnation of the practice by shaking out the folds of his garments. Since the folds near the waist were used as pockets, this gesture was the equivalent of us turning our pockets inside out to show that we don't have even a penny in them. Here the action was a dramatic way of symbolizing the judgment that God would bring on those who oppressed the poor.

Some commentators have interpreted Nehemiah's statement that he too had been lending money as an admission of guilt and a promise of repentance on his part. But in light of his self-defense that follows, it seems more likely that he was holding himself up as an example of one who was following the law and not charging interest. Nehemiah's strong words had the desired effect. The leaders promised to end the exploitation that was threatening the restoration of the nation.

The Old Testament passages that condemned the taking of interest, or at least excessive interest, have often caused Christians to ask if all receiving of interest is still wrong today. Even in the Old Testament the taking of interest was not completely forbidden: "You may charge a foreigner interest, but not a brother Israelite" (Deuteronomy 23:20). What God had forbidden was interest on loans made to fellow Israelites for the necessities of life.

Nor should we exploit people's misfortunes for financial gain. When people have suffered severe losses and cannot provide the food, clothing, shelter, and medical care their families need, we should gladly loan or give them what they need without concern of gain for ourselves. Jesus tells us: "And if you lend to those from whom you expect repayment, what credit is that to you? . . . But love your enemies, do good to them, and lend to them without expecting to get anything back" (Luke 6:34,35). Yes, we are even to give to our enemies!

Most loans today are not made for the necessities of life, but are used as capital to make profits for the borrower or to improve his standard of living. The Bible does not specifically deal with such loans and interest. Jesus mentions the practice in one of his parables. There the master tells his servant who wasted his money, "You should have put my money on deposit with the bankers, so that when I returned I would have received it back with interest" (Matthew 25:27). If anything, Jesus seems to endorse the practice, rather than condemn it. But because he is merely using the practice to illustrate a story, we can't read too much into his words.

Although the Bible does not directly speak to the topic of loans, it does leave us with two principles to follow. On the one hand, we are to do everything in our power to help those in real need. On the other hand, we are not to encourage the laziness of parasites who would live off the labors of others. Saint Paul set down this rule against laziness: "If a man will not work, he shall not eat" (2 Thessalonians 3:6-13; also 2 Corinthians 8:13-15). These principles will help guide us in using the possessions God has entrusted to us.

Nehemiah's self-defense

¹⁴Moreover, from the twentieth year of King Artaxerxes, when I was appointed to be their governor in the land of Judah, until his thirty-second year—twelve years—neither I nor my brothers ate the food allotted to the governor. ¹⁵But the earlier governors—those preceding me—placed a heavy burden on the people and took forty shekels of silver from them in addition to food and wine. Their assistants also lorded it over the people. But out of reverence for God I did not act like that. ¹⁶Instead, I devoted myself to the work on this wall. All my men were assembled there for the work; we did not acquire any land.

¹⁷Furthermore, a hundred and fifty Jews and officials ate at my table, as well as those who came to us from the surrounding nations. ¹⁸Each day one ox, six choice sheep and some poultry were prepared for me, and every ten days an abundant supply of wine of all kinds. In spite of all this, I never demanded the food allotted to the governor, because the demands were heavy on these people.

¹⁹Remember me with favor, O my God, for all I have done for these people.

This section of Scripture has troubled commentators because it covers a span of 12 years (445–433 B.C.); but the wall seems to have been completed in less than two months, shortly after Nehemiah's return (Nehemiah 6:15). There is no problem or contradiction here. Nehemiah undoubtedly compiled his memoirs at the end of his career. Here he was simply stating that the same unselfish service that characterized his actions during the building project in the first year of his administration was maintained throughout his term of office. He was not saying that it took 12 years to build the wall.

When King Artaxerxes authorized Nehemiah to go to Judah, he apparently gave him a relatively short leave of absence.

Nehemiah's stay in Jerusalem must have extended far beyond his original expectation, for he was in Judah for 12 years. When Nehemiah wrote his memoirs at the end of his career, he defended himself against enemies in much the same fashion as Saint Paul does in 2 Corinthians. Nehemiah did this so that his administration would not be discredited. He refuted the charge that he had exploited the people and was in the work for his own gain; he pointed out that he did not even take the governor's pay he was entitled to. On the contrary, he used his own money to pay for the entertaining and receptions that his position required. Because he realized that he was a servant of God, Nehemiah did not lord it over God's people or demand his rights and prerogatives as governor. Instead, he conducted himself unselfishly and looked first to the interests of the people he was sent to serve.

In this respect Nehemiah is an example to believers today. We also have the greater example of our Lord Jesus, who did not come to be served, but to serve and give his life as a ransom for many. The sacrifices we make deserve no reward; we are only doing our duty. Yet, like Nehemiah, we can be confident that God will remember and reward our faithfulness. This confidence is well founded, for we have such a promise from Christ: "If anyone gives a cup of cold water to one of these little ones because he is my disciple, I tell you the truth, he will certainly not lose his reward" (Matthew 10:42).

More opposition from outside

6 **When word came to Sanballat, Tobiah, Geshem the Arab and the rest of our enemies that I had rebuilt the wall and not a gap was left in it—though up to that time I had not set the doors in the gates—²Sanballat and Geshem sent me a message: "Come, let us meet together in one of the villages on the plain of Ono."**

But they were scheming to harm me; ³so I sent messengers to them with this reply: "I am carrying on a great project and cannot go down. Why should the work stop while I leave it and go down to you?" ⁴Four times they sent me the same message, and each time I gave them the same answer.

⁵Then, the fifth time, Sanballat sent his aide to me with the same message, and in his hand was an unsealed letter ⁶in which was written:

"It is reported among the nations—and Geshem says it is true—that you and the Jews are plotting to revolt, and therefore you are building the wall. Moreover, according to these reports you are about to become their king ⁷and have even appointed prophets to make this proclamation about you in Jerusalem: 'There is a king in Judah!' Now this report will get back to the king; so come, let us confer together."

⁸I sent him this reply: "Nothing like what you are saying is happening; you are just making it up out of your head."

⁹They were all trying to frighten us, thinking, "Their hands will get too weak for the work, and it will not be completed."

But I prayed, "Now strengthen my hands."

The same cowardly opposition we noted earlier has surfaced again. Sanballat and his gang tried to lure Nehemiah to Ono so they could kidnap or kill him and thus stop the work. Ono was a town about 25 miles northwest of Jerusalem, where the borders of Judea, Samaria, and Philistia met. It was probably a neutral site for a meeting. In spite of the enemies' persistence, Nehemiah refused to fall for their trick.

Sanballat made one last attempt. He pretended that he wanted to help Nehemiah stop the rumors that Nehemiah was preparing a revolt against Persia. Sanballat implied there might be some basis for believing such rumors. After all, why else would Nehemiah be building a wall? With "good neighbors" like Sanballat and Geshem, surely

Nehemiah would have no need for a wall, except to revolt against Persia.

Nehemiah could well have been concerned that such rumors would alarm the king. Revolts were common in the Persian Empire, and most were led by trusted associates of the king. But Nehemiah knew there could be only one source for such rumors—Sanballat and his friends. If Sanballat had any concern for helping Nehemiah put an end to rumors, he certainly would not have sent a letter accusing Nehemiah of treason, unsealed and open for anyone to read!

The last sentence of this section is obscure in the Hebrew; it does not indicate who is saying the words. The NIV appropriately translates it as a short prayer of Nehemiah, since such prayers were typical of him. His response was to ignore the lies of the enemy, continue his work, and leave his defense to the Lord.

This can be a lesson for us. We too may experience slander and attacks as we take unpopular positions because of loyalty to God's Word. At times we may need to refute such attacks, as Paul did in 2 Corinthians 10–12, so that people are not misled by them. But we should not allow petty attacks to divert us from our great project of spreading the gospel. If we spend so much time trying to refute attacks that we divert a great deal of time and energy from preaching the gospel, God's enemies have accomplished their purpose. Rather, let us devote our resources and energy primarily to the task of building through the gospel. We need not be distressed by the slander of enemies. The only verdict on our work that counts is God's. We can follow Nehemiah's example and busy ourselves with the assignment God has given us and leave our defense to him.

The enemies inside join the enemies from outside

¹⁰**One day I went to the house of Shemaiah son of Delaiah, the son of Mehetabel, who was shut in at his home. He said, "Let us meet in the house of God, inside the temple, and let us close the temple doors, because men are coming to kill you—by night they are coming to kill you."**

¹¹**But I said, "Should a man like me run away? Or should one like me go into the temple to save his life? I will not go!"** ¹²**I realized that God had not sent him, but that he had prophesied against me because Tobiah and Sanballat had hired him.** ¹³**He had been hired to intimidate me so that I would commit a sin by doing this, and then they would give me a bad name to discredit me.**

¹⁴**Remember Tobiah and Sanballat, O my God, because of what they have done; remember also the prophetess Noadiah and the rest of the prophets who have been trying to intimidate me.**

When pressure from outside failed, the enemies tried to apply pressure through their allies in Jerusalem. Nehemiah's aid to the oppressed, which we heard about in chapter 5, may have been one reason that some of the upper class in Judah worked to undermine his leadership. Marriage and commercial alliances with the neighboring peoples were additional causes of this treachery. The enemies reached a new low when they recruited false prophets to try to deceive Nehemiah. Such false prophets were nothing new. They had often opposed the leaders sent by God. This was especially true at the time of Jeremiah when he was warning the people of the fall of Jerusalem. Jeremiah chapter 23 describes the false prophets in detail: "'I did not send or appoint them. They do not benefit these people in the least,' declares the LORD" (verse 32).

Some commentators maintain that the temptation was for Nehemiah to enter an area of the temple restricted to priests. Nehemiah's reply, however, seems to indicate that he was being urged to follow the ancient practice of seeking sanctuary from danger in the temple. Since prophets sometimes acted out their prophecies, Shemaiah's being "shut in" may refer to some symbolic act that he was performing to urge Nehemiah to seek refuge in the temple. Such flight would have been wrong because Nehemiah would be deserting his followers, who were daily exposed to danger on the walls. If Nehemiah were afraid to face the enemies, why should his followers face them? But Nehemiah rejected the temptation. And, as he had done so often, he entrusted his case to God in prayer.

The wall completed despite opposition

¹⁵**So the wall was completed on the twenty-fifth of Elul, in fifty-two days. ¹⁶When all our enemies heard about this, all the surrounding nations were afraid and lost their self-confidence, because they realized that this work had been done with the help of our God.**

¹⁷**Also, in those days the nobles of Judah were sending many letters to Tobiah, and replies from Tobiah kept coming to them. ¹⁸For many in Judah were under oath to him, since he was son-in-law to Shecaniah son of Arah, and his son Jehohanan had married the daughter of Meshullam son of Berekiah. ¹⁹Moreover, they kept reporting to me his good deeds and then telling him what I said. And Tobiah sent letters to intimidate me.**

7 **After the wall had been rebuilt and I had set the doors in place, the gatekeepers and the singers and the Levites were appointed. ²I put in charge of Jerusalem my brother Hanani, along with Hananiah the commander of the citadel, because he was a man of integrity and feared God more than most men do. ³I said to them, "The gates of Jerusalem are not to be opened until the sun is hot. While the gatekeepers are still on duty, have them shut the doors and bar them. Also appoint residents of Jerusalem as guards, some at their posts and some near their own houses."**

Despite all the schemes of the enemy, the reconstruction of the walls took less than two months. Elul is a fall month, roughly equal to October. It appears that the wall was finished within six months after Nehemiah's departure from Persia in the spring month of Nisan.

Even as the walls were being completed, opposition from outside and inside Jerusalem continued. This section is especially important to the overall theme of Ezra and Nehemiah because it demonstrates that the intermarriages with heathen neighbors were actually undermining the strength of the nation. When Ezra and Nehemiah denounced such intermarriage, they were not just arguing about unimportant religious distinction or personal prejudices. They were dealing with a real threat to Israel. Leading citizens in Judah were so compromised by their commercial and marital ties with heathen neighbors that they were unable to see any reason why Tobiah should not be accepted as one of them. He had even been provided a room in the temple (Nehemiah 13:4-9)! The completion of the walls did not stop the evil effects of these intermarriages.

Nehemiah now turned his attention to organizing an orderly administration of the restored city. Two reliable, godly men were entrusted with governing the city. Nehemiah's brother Hanani seems to have filled a position similar to that of our mayors. Hananiah was responsible for military and police operations in the city. Strong security measures and military alertness had to continue, since a sneak attack was still a possibility. The appointment of gatekeepers, singers, and Levites could refer to preparations for the dedication ceremonies described in Nehemiah chapter 12. It might also refer to the appointing of additional temple workers because of the planned increase of population in Jerusalem and the expanded temple services that would result.

Now that the walls were completed, Nehemiah faced the job of repopulating the city. He needed a census to choose new inhabitants for the city. The completion of this project is reported in Nehemiah chapter 11. While preparing for this redistribution of population, Nehemiah found a list of the families who had returned with Zerubbabel son of Shealtiel in the first return nearly one hundred years earlier. Because he decided to follow the arrangement of this list for his own census, Nehemiah included it in his memoirs as it is recorded in 7:4-73. This list is almost the same as the list of returnees published in Ezra chapter 2. Nevertheless, there are some puzzling differences in names and numbers. Since we have already discussed the basic organization of the list in the commentary on Ezra chapter 2, we will not discuss it again here. In the reproduction of Nehemiah's list that follows, the main phrases in which Nehemiah's list differs from Ezra's are indicated in italics. Asterisks indicate points at which Nehemiah has omitted material from Ezra. These markings will make it easier for you to compare the two lists if you choose to do so. After presenting the list, we will try to account for these discrepancies.

The list of exiles who returned

⁴Now the city was large and spacious, but there were few people in it, and the houses had not yet been rebuilt. ⁵So my God put it into my heart to assemble the nobles, the officials and the common people for registration by families. I found the genealogical record of those who had been the first to return. This is what I found written there:

⁶These are the people of the province who came up from the captivity of the exiles, whom Nebuchadnezzar king of Babylon had taken captive* (they returned to Jerusalem and Judah, each to his own town, ⁷in company with Zerubbabel, Jeshua, Nehemiah, *Azariah, Raamiah, Nahamani,* Mordecai, Bilshan, *Mispereth,* Bigvai, *Nehum* and Baanah):

The list of the men of Israel:

[8]the descendants of Parosh	2,172
[9] of Shephatiah	372
[10]of Arah	652
[11]of Pahath-Moab (through the line of Jeshua and Joab)	2,818
[12]of Elam	1,254
[13]of Zattu	845
[14]of Zaccai	760
[15]of *Binnui*	*648*
[16]of Bebai	*628*
[17]of Azgad	*2,322*
[18]of Adonikam	*667*
[19]of Bigvai	*2,067*
[20]of Adin	*655*
[21]of Ater (through Hezekiah)	98
[22]of Hashum	*328*
[23]of Bezai	*324*
[24]of *Hariph*	112
[25]of *Gibeon*	95
[26]the men of Bethlehem and Netophah	*188*
[27]of Anathoth	128
[28]of Beth Azmaveth	42
[29]of Kiriath Jearim, Kephirah and Beeroth	743
[30]of Ramah and Geba	621
[31]of Micmash	122
[32]of Bethel and Ai	123
[33]of *the other* Nebo	52*
[34]of the other Elam	1,254
[35]of Harim	320
[36]of Jericho	345
[37]of Lod, Hadid and Ono	721
[38]of Senaah	*3,930*

[39]The priests:

the descendants of Jedaiah (through the family of Jeshua)	973

[40]of Immer	1,052
[41]of Pashhur	1,247
[42]of Harim	1,017

[43]The Levites:

the descendants of Jeshua (*through* Kadmiel
through the line of Hodaviah) 74

[44]The singers:

the descendants of Asaph 148

[45]The gatekeepers:*

the descendants of
Shallum, Ater,
Talmon, Akkub, Hatita and Shobai *138*

[46]The temple servants:

the descendants of
Ziha, Hasupha, Tabbaoth,
[47]Keros, *Sia,* Padon,
[48]Lebana, Hagaba,* Shalmai,
[49]Hanan, Giddel, *Gahar,*
[50]Reaiah, Rezin, Nekoda,
[51]Gazzam, Uzza, Paseah,
[52]Besai,* Meunim, Nephussim,
[53]Bakbuk, Hakupha, Harhur,
[54]Bazluth, Mehida, Harsha,
[55]Barkos, Sisera, Temah,
[56]Neziah and Hatipha

[57]The descendants of the servants of Solomon:

the descendants of
Sotai, *Sophereth, Perida,*
[58]Jaala, Darkon, Giddel,
[59]Shephatiah, Hattil,
Pokereth-Hazzebaim and *Amon*

[60]The temple servants and the descendants of the
servants of Solomon 392

[61]The following came up from the towns of Tel Melah, Tel
Harsha, Kerub, Addon and Immer, but they could not show
that their families were descended from Israel:

[62]the descendants of
Delaiah, Tobiah and Nekoda 642

[63]And from among the priests:

the descendants of
Hobaiah, Hakkoz and Barzillai (a man who had

married a daughter of Barzillai the Gileadite and was called by that name).

⁶⁴These searched for their family records, but they could not find them and so were excluded from the priesthood as unclean. ⁶⁵The governor, therefore, ordered them not to eat any of the most sacred food until there should be a priest ministering with the Urim and Thummim.

⁶⁶The whole company numbered 42,360, ⁶⁷besides their 7,337 menservants and maidservants; and they also had 245 men and women singers. ⁶⁸There were 736 horses, 245 mules, ⁶⁹435 camels and 6,720 donkeys.

⁷⁰*Some of the heads of the families contributed to the work. The governor gave to the treasury 1,000 drachmas of gold, 50 bowls and 530 garments for priests. ⁷¹Some of the heads of the families gave to the treasury for the work 20,000 drachmas of gold and 2,200 minas of silver. ⁷²The total given by the rest of the people was 20,000 drachmas of gold, 2,000 minas of silver and 67 garments for priests.*

⁷³The priests, the Levites, *the gatekeepers, the singers* and the temple servants, along with certain of the people and the rest of the Israelites, settled in their own towns.

One might wonder whether it's worth the time and bother to compare the differences between this list and the list in Ezra. A comparison might be unnecessary if there were no critics waiting to pounce on alleged errors in the Bible. Critics point to "discrepancies" between the two lists in their efforts to discredit the doctrine of biblical inerrancy. In the face of such attacks on the Bible, we must take time to study the issue.

Out of necessity this study will become a bit technical. As you read the following comments, try to concentrate on the basic principles without getting bogged down in details.

How shall we explain the discrepancies between these two lists? Many of the names are identical, and the wording and arrangement of the two lists is so very close. It seems certain that they describe the same period of Israel's history and that the two lists are derived from the same written source. It does not seem plausible to claim these are two different lists, which just happen to have some of the same names. They are clearly variant forms of the same basic list.

What are some of the disagreements between the two lists? First of all, many of the names in Nehemiah are not the same as those in Ezra. In a few cases this happens even when the numbers following the names at a certain position in the list are the same (Jorah/Hariph and Gibeon/Gibbar). In most cases the names are close enough that they can be recognized as variants of the same name (Bani/Binnui, Mispar/Mispereth, Amon/Ami, Sia/Siaha, and so on). This is no different than what we do in English (John/Johnny, Richard/Rich/Rick/Dick, Margaret/Maggie/Marge/Meg). People sometimes go by one name in their family and by a different name among their friends or business associates. The discrepancy of names between the two lists need not disturb us; it has nothing to do with the inerrancy of Scripture. Two versions of the list, made at different times, simply use different forms of the same names.

In a few cases it is possible that copying errors may have crept into the text of either Ezra or Nehemiah (Nehum/Rehum). Inspiration applies only to the writing of the original manuscripts, not to the copying. There may be occasional copying mistakes in our copies of the Bible, but none of them affect any doctrine or teaching of the Bible.

Nehemiah omits some of the items in Ezra and occasionally changes the order of names. Since both lists are summaries, not complete lists, these are simply variations, not errors. Both lists give the total number of returnees as 42,360. But Ezra lists only 29,818 returnees and Nehemiah only 31,818 in their lists of specific families. Neither list attempts to list every returnee, so it is not surprising that there is some difference in the number of names listed.

It is more difficult to explain the discrepancies in the numbers for the same family. For example, Ezra says there were 775 returnees from the family of Arah, but Nehemiah lists only 652. Many similar discrepancies are marked in the previous text (verses 4-73). In general, the numbers in Nehemiah tend to be larger than the corresponding numbers in Ezra, but this is not always the case. It is possible that there may be a few copying errors in one of the texts as we have it today, but this is not an adequate explanation for the differences. It is more probable that Ezra and Nehemiah simply used lists from different stages of the original census. From Ezra chapter 2 we learned that some people had difficulty proving their descent. A number of people not in the first listing may have been added after they had successfully demonstrated their ancestry.

Whatever other reasons there may be for the variations in the two lists, they can all be explained by the suggestion that the lists of Ezra and Nehemiah are simply two different stages of the same basic census. Each man was satisfied to use the list as he found it, since his goal was to provide a basic outline of the returnees, not to list every person. Although we do not have enough information to demonstrate with certainty how the two lists originated, we do see that they can be adequately explained without accusing either Ezra or Nehemiah of error.

PART TWO

Rebuilding the Spiritual Walls of Jerusalem
(8:1–13:31)

After Nehemiah had rebuilt the walls of Jerusalem to provide physical security for the people of Judah, he had to take steps to strengthen the nation's spiritual security. He accomplished this by promoting religious reforms under the priest Ezra.

Ezra had returned to Jerusalem more than ten years before Nehemiah returned. At that time he had taken action to put an end to the practice of intermarriage with heathen neighbors (Ezra 9,10). We know nothing of his activities during the ten years after his first reform.

Ezra's first appearance in the book of Nehemiah is in chapter 8. Because this section is written in the style of Ezra, critics have claimed that it is out of place in the memoirs of Nehemiah. Some have suggested that Nehemiah chapters 8 to 10 belong at the end of Ezra or in some other place. There is no need, however, to chop up the book of Nehemiah or to rearrange it. It is possible that Nehemiah himself inserted Ezra's account of these religious reforms at this point. If Nehemiah himself is the author of the book of Nehemiah, there is no reason he could not have used Ezra's memoirs as a source. Or if Ezra wrote the book of Nehemiah, using Nehemiah's memoirs as his primary source, he could well have inserted an account of his own role in Nehemiah's administration.

It appears that almost all the events described in the book of Nehemiah took place in the fall of Nehemiah's first year in Jerusalem, within a few weeks after the completion of the city walls. The only exceptions to this are a few summary remarks written after Nehemiah's retirement and the reforms and lists of Nehemiah chapter 13.

Ezra reads the law

When the seventh month came and the Israelites had settled in their towns,

8 ¹all the people assembled as one man in the square before the Water Gate. They told Ezra the scribe to bring out the Book of the Law of Moses, which the LORD had commanded for Israel.

²So on the first day of the seventh month Ezra the priest brought the Law before the assembly, which was made up of men and women and all who were able to understand. ³He read it aloud from daybreak till noon as he faced the square before the Water Gate in the presence of the men, women and others who could understand. And all the people listened attentively to the Book of the Law.

⁴Ezra the scribe stood on a high wooden platform built for the occasion. Beside him on the right stood Mattithiah, Shema, Anaiah, Uriah, Hilkiah and Maaseiah; and on his left were Pedaiah, Mishael, Malkijah, Hashum, Hashbaddanah, Zechariah and Meshullam.

⁵Ezra opened the book. All the people could see him because he was standing above them; and as he opened it, the people all stood up. ⁶Ezra praised the LORD, the great God; and all the people lifted their hands and responded, "Amen! Amen!" Then they bowed down and worshiped the LORD with their faces to the ground.

⁷The Levites—Jeshua, Bani, Sherebiah, Jamin, Akkub, Shabbethai, Hodiah, Maaseiah, Kelita, Azariah, Jozabad, Hanan and Pelaiah—instructed the people in the Law while the people were standing there. ⁸They read from the Book of the Law of God, making it clear

and giving the meaning so that the people could understand what was being read.

The celebration in the seventh month reminds us of the similar celebration at the time of Zerubbabel's return one hundred years earlier. The first day of the seventh month was the civil New Year's Day, the Feast of Trumpets. This celebration went back to the time of Moses: "The LORD said to Moses, 'Say to the Israelites: "On the first day of the seventh month you are to have a day of rest, a sacred assembly commemorated with trumpet blasts"'" (Leviticus 23:23,24; also Numbers 29:1-6).

The people assembled in the public square near the Water Gate on the east side of the city. Men, women, and children old enough to understand all listened attentively as Ezra read from the Law. "The Book of the Law" undoubtedly refers to parts of the five books of Moses (Genesis–Deuteronomy). Most likely Ezra read the passages in Exodus and Deuteronomy that describe God's establishment of his covenant with Israel.

Ezra was assisted in this work by two groups of people. The role of the 13 men who stood beside him on the speaker's platform is not specified. They may have been prominent priests or laymen who stood beside Ezra as a demonstration of support, much in the same way that dignitaries share the platform with a president or governor today. The second group, the Levites, assisted Ezra in the actual teaching of the Word. It is not clear whether they took turns with Ezra in the reading or simply reread and explained portions of the text to smaller groups of people after Ezra had read to the whole group. Part of their explanation of the Scriptures may have been translating them into Aramaic for those who no longer understood the biblical Hebrew well.

The people responded with praise and repentance. The following verses tell us that the people wept during the reading, so it must have included portions of Moses' writings that rebuked Israel's sin. When the people of Israel examined themselves, they realized they had been unfaithful. They wept tears of repentance. The preaching of God's law had achieved its intended purpose when it aroused an awareness of sin, but the assurance of forgiveness and mercy would soon bring joy to replace the tears.

In our day, as in Nehemiah's, the revival of spiritual life must begin with the preaching of law and gospel. This alone can produce renewal through confession and absolution.

The people rejoice

⁹**Then Nehemiah the governor, Ezra the priest and scribe, and the Levites who were instructing the people said to them all, "This day is sacred to the LORD your God. Do not mourn or weep." For all the people had been weeping as they listened to the words of the Law.**

¹⁰**Nehemiah said, "Go and enjoy choice food and sweet drinks, and send some to those who have nothing prepared. This day is sacred to our Lord. Do not grieve, for the joy of the LORD is your strength."**

¹¹**The Levites calmed all the people, saying, "Be still, for this is a sacred day. Do not grieve."**

¹²**Then all the people went away to eat and drink, to send portions of food and to celebrate with great joy, because they now understood the words that had been made known to them.**

Ecclesiastes tells us there is "a time to weep and a time to laugh, a time to mourn and a time to dance" (3:4). There are appropriate times to mourn over our sins. In our worship calendar, Ash Wednesday and Good Friday are such days. On the other hand, there are times when such sorrow and gloom are inappropriate. Christmas and Easter are such days. On these festivals a joyful celebration of God's goodness is appropriate. During Old Testament times, Israel had an appropriate day for mourning and repentance—the Day of Atonement on the tenth day of the seventh month. The Feast of Trumpets, however, was to be a day of joy.

On this day God's people had just had the opportunity to hear God's Word and to be reassured of God's loving design for them. Although they wept when they recognized their sinful shortcomings, Nehemiah reminded them that this was a day to rejoice. He urged the people to express their joy in an appropriate way with special holiday meals and by sharing their abundance with the less fortunate.

Some Christians have frowned on holidays like Christmas and Easter and the accompanying festivities. But festive meals and celebrations are appropriate—as long as these festivities direct our attention to the Lord, rather than away from him. The Holy Scriptures often describe eternal life as a feast. Our feasts on earth should remind us of that infinitely more blessed feast to come. God has showered rich material blessings on us. It's appropriate to use them with joy and thanksgiving. "A man can do nothing better than to eat and drink and find satisfaction in his work. This . . . is from the hand of God, for without him, who can eat or find enjoyment?" (Ecclesiastes 2:24,25). Christ, the heavenly Bridegroom, has come. Let us celebrate his coming with rejoicing! As Christ himself asks, "How can the guests of the bridegroom mourn while he is with them?" (Matthew 9:15).

The people celebrate

¹³On the second day of the month, the heads of all the families, along with the priests and the Levites, gathered around Ezra

the scribe to give attention to the words of the Law. ¹⁴**They found written in the Law, which the** Lord **had commanded through Moses, that the Israelites were to live in booths during the feast of the seventh month** ¹⁵**and that they should proclaim this word and spread it throughout their towns and in Jerusalem: "Go out into the hill country and bring back branches from olive and wild olive trees, and from myrtles, palms and shade trees, to make booths"— as it is written.**

¹⁶**So the people went out and brought back branches and built themselves booths on their own roofs, in their courtyards, in the courts of the house of God and in the square by the Water Gate and the one by the Gate of Ephraim.** ¹⁷**The whole company that had returned from exile built booths and lived in them. From the days of Joshua son of Nun until that day, the Israelites had not celebrated it like this. And their joy was very great.**

¹⁸**Day after day, from the first day to the last, Ezra read from the Book of the Law of God. They celebrated the feast for seven days, and on the eighth day, in accordance with the regulation, there was an assembly.**

The second day of the seventh month was not a holiday, but the leaders of the people continued their special Bible study. This study led to the rediscovery of the rules for celebrating the Feast of Tabernacles, or Booths (Leviticus 23:33-44). Apparently there had been a terrible neglect in the celebration of this feast, although we know it was celebrated at least once in the days of Zerubbabel (Ezra 3:4). At that time there was no specific mention of the booths, so perhaps it was especially that aspect of the feast that had fallen into disuse.

The booths were intended to remind the Israelites of the years when they had lived in temporary shelters in the wilderness. This holiday was also a joyous autumn harvest festival. In Deuteronomy 31:10,11 the reading of the law is specified as a chief feature of this festival: "At the end of every seven years, in the year for canceling debts, during the Feast of the Tabernacles, . . . you shall read this law." Nehemiah emphasized the people's return to the study of God's Word during this feast.

In a way it is surprising that there is no mention of the solemn Day of Atonement, which also occurred in the seventh month. Perhaps this is due to the desire to emphasize joyous festivals.

Ezra's restoration of the Feast of Tabernacles is described as the most outstanding celebration of this feast since the days of Joshua. This comment probably refers to the degree to which the whole nation flocked to Jerusalem and built booths in every available open space. There certainly was special cause for joy now that the walls of Jerusalem had been restored. The extensive reading of the law, which continued throughout the seven days of the festival, was a vital step in rebuilding the spiritual strength of the nation. Further steps in renewing the nation's dedication to the Lord would follow this good beginning.

The Israelites make a covenant with the Lord

The Levites prepare the people

9 **On the twenty-fourth day of the same month, the Israelites gathered together, fasting and wearing sackcloth and having dust on their heads. ²Those of Israelite descent had separated themselves from all foreigners. They stood in their places and confessed their sins and the wickedness of their fathers. ³They stood where they were and read from the Book of the Law of the LORD their God for a quarter of the day, and spent another quarter of the day in confession and in worshiping the LORD their God. ⁴Standing on the stairs were the Levites—Jeshua, Bani, Kadmiel, Shebaniah, Bunni, Sherebiah, Bani and Kenani—who called with loud voices to the LORD their God. ⁵And the Levites—Jeshua, Kadmiel, Bani, Hashabneiah, Sherebiah, Hodiah, Shebaniah and**

Pethahiah—said: "Stand up and praise the LORD your God, who is from everlasting to everlasting."

After the joyful celebration of the Feast of Trumpets and the Feast of Tabernacles, the people returned to a consideration of their sins. They observed a day of repentance to prepare for renewing their commitment to the Lord. The 24th day of the seventh month was not a holiday prescribed by the Law of Moses. The Day of Atonement, the main penitential day of the Old Testament worship calendar, was supposed to be celebrated on the tenth day of the seventh month. Since it is not mentioned here, perhaps it had not been properly observed and this day of repentance was taking its place.

The people prepared to reaffirm the Sinaitic covenant by fasting and wearing sackcloth and ashes, which symbolized humility and repentance. A survival of these symbols of repentance is the practice, observed by some Christians, of wearing ashes on Ash Wednesday and fasting during Lent. Separation from foreigners and hearing God's law were other preparations for renewing the covenant. It is not clear if the separation from foreigners refers to new reforms or to the earlier reforms of Ezra.

Two groups of Levites led the worship service that prepared the people to renew their covenant with the Lord. One group led in prayer; the other group chanted or recited a penitential psalm that reviewed the history of God's relationship with Israel. This psalm, which will take up the remainder of Nehemiah chapter 9, contrasts God's goodness with Israel's continued disobedience and unfaithfulness. It emphasizes God's covenant with Abraham, a gospel covenant based on God's grace and on the promise of the coming Savior. It was not a legal covenant that depended on the people's obedience, as did the covenant made through Moses. At Mount Sinai the Israelites had promised

119

to obey the Law (Exodus 24). They had renewed that promise when they entered the Promised Land (Joshua 24). Because they had not lived up to these promises, the people could not appeal to the covenant of Sinai as they asked God for help. They had not kept their part of that bargain. Their only hope, then, was the Lord's mercy and faithfulness to the gospel promise he had first delivered to Abraham.

This truth is the theme of the psalm that the Levites recited. Their psalm is similar to other historical psalms with a penitential theme, such as Psalms 78, 105, and 106. The Septuagint, a very ancient Greek translation of the Old Testament, lists Ezra as the author of the psalm in our text. Since it is similar to Ezra's prayer in Ezra chapter 9, this is a plausible suggestion. Because this psalm sweeps through the whole of Old Testament history, it will not be possible to comment on it in detail here. Instead, we will let it speak for itself. The headings added to the psalm include the main Scripture passages summarized in each section of the psalm. You may read these passages for further information about the historical circumstances described in each section of the psalm. A few of the more obscure references will be briefly discussed in the commentary following the psalm. But our primary interest is the central theme of the psalm: the contrast between God's faithfulness to his gospel promise and the Israelites' unfaithfulness to their promise to serve and obey God.

The people remember God's goodness
in their early history

God's goodness in creation
(Genesis 1,2)

"Blessed be your glorious name, and may it be exalted above all blessing and praise. ⁶You alone are the LORD. You

made the heavens, even the highest heavens, and all their starry host, the earth and all that is on it, the seas and all that is in them. You give life to everything, and the multitudes of heaven worship you.

God's goodness in calling Abraham
(Genesis 12,15)

⁷"You are the Lᴏʀᴅ God, who chose Abram and brought him out of Ur of the Chaldeans and named him Abraham. ⁸You found his heart faithful to you, and you made a covenant with him to give to his descendants the land of the Canaanites, Hittites, Amorites, Perizzites, Jebusites and Girgashites. You have kept your promise because you are righteous.

God's goodness in leading the people out of Egypt
(Exodus 4–15)

⁹"You saw the suffering of our forefathers in Egypt; you heard their cry at the Red Sea. ¹⁰You sent miraculous signs and wonders against Pharaoh, against all his officials and all the people of his land, for you knew how arrogantly the Egyptians treated them. You made a name for yourself, which remains to this day. ¹¹You divided the sea before them, so that they passed through it on dry ground, but you hurled their pursuers into the depths, like a stone into mighty waters. ¹²By day you led them with a pillar of cloud, and by night with a pillar of fire to give them light on the way they were to take.

God's care for them in the wilderness
(Exodus 20,16,17)

¹³"You came down on Mount Sinai; you spoke to them from heaven. You gave them regulations and laws that are just and right, and decrees and commands that are good. ¹⁴You made known to them your holy Sabbath and gave them commands,

decrees and laws through your servant Moses. ¹⁵In their hunger you gave them bread from heaven and in their thirst you brought them water from the rock; you told them to go in and take possession of the land you had sworn with uplifted hand to give to them.

Israel's rebellion and God's mercy
(Exodus 32–34; Numbers 11–16; Deuteronomy 4–9)

¹⁶"But they, our forefathers, became arrogant and stiff-necked, and did not obey your commands. ¹⁷They refused to listen and failed to remember the miracles you performed among them. They became stiff-necked and in their rebellion appointed a leader in order to return to their slavery. But you are a forgiving God, gracious and compassionate, slow to anger and abounding in love. Therefore you did not desert them, ¹⁸even when they cast for themselves an image of a calf and said, 'This is your god, who brought you up out of Egypt,' or when they committed awful blasphemies.

¹⁹"Because of your great compassion you did not abandon them in the desert. By day the pillar of cloud did not cease to guide them on their path, nor the pillar of fire by night to shine on the way they were to take. ²⁰You gave your good Spirit to instruct them. You did not withhold your manna from their mouths, and you gave them water for their thirst. ²¹For forty years you sustained them in the desert; they lacked nothing, their clothes did not wear out nor did their feet become swollen.

This first section of the psalm reviews God's goodness from creation until Israel's entry into the land of Canaan. Although the Lord had demonstrated his goodness in so many ways, Israel spent the whole 40 years in the wilderness complaining and rebelling. The even rejected Moses as their leader and chose Korah to lead them back to Egypt. As a result, the whole generation that had left Egypt, except for Caleb and Joshua, perished in the wilderness. In spite of

Israel's ingratitude, the Lord kept this covenant. He led the next generation into the Promised Land. Nevertheless, once the people were safely established in the land, they again forgot their promise to God.

The people remember God's continued goodness in the land

God's goodness during the conquest
(Numbers 21; Joshua 6–11)

²²"You gave them kingdoms and nations, allotting to them even the remotest frontiers. They took over the country of Sihon king of Heshbon and the country of Og king of Bashan. ²³You made their sons as numerous as the stars in the sky, and you brought them into the land that you told their fathers to enter and possess. ²⁴Their sons went in and took possession of the land. You subdued before them the Canaanites, who lived in the land; you handed the Canaanites over to them, along with their kings and the peoples of the land, to deal with them as they pleased. ²⁵They captured fortified cities and fertile land; they took possession of houses filled with all kinds of good things, wells already dug, vineyards, olive groves and fruit trees in abundance. They ate to the full and were well-nourished; they reveled in your great goodness.

Israel forgets God's goodness
(Judges 2,3)

²⁶"But they were disobedient and rebelled against you; they put your law behind their backs. They killed your prophets, who had admonished them in order to turn them back to you; they committed awful blasphemies. ²⁷So you handed them over to their enemies, who oppressed them. But when they were oppressed they cried out to you. From heaven you heard them, and in your great compassion you gave them deliverers, who rescued them from the hand of their enemies.

²⁸**"But as soon as they were at rest, they again did what was evil in your sight. Then you abandoned them to the hand of their enemies so that they ruled over them. And when they cried out to you again, you heard from heaven, and in your compassion you delivered them time after time.**

²⁹**"You warned them to return to your law, but they became arrogant and disobeyed your commands. They sinned against your ordinances, by which a man will live if he obeys them. Stubbornly they turned their backs on you, became stiff-necked and refused to listen.** ³⁰**For many years you were patient with them. By your Spirit you admonished them through your prophets. Yet they paid no attention, so you handed them over to the neighboring peoples.** ³¹**But in your great mercy you did not put an end to them, or abandon them, for you are a gracious and merciful God.**

This section of the psalm summarizes all the history in the books of Judges, 1 and 2 Samuel, and 1 and 2 Kings. God had begun to give the Israelites victories even before they crossed the Jordan River, when he gave them the land of Sihon and Og, east of the Jordan. Then, in the battles of Jericho and Aijalon when he made the sun stand still, he gave them their promised homeland (Joshua 6,10). Nevertheless, the people soon forgot him and turned to Baal and other gods. In spite of this, when they repented, God sent judges like Gideon, Deborah, and Samson to deliver the people. Even Saul, who turned out to be an ungodly king, led them to many victories over their enemies. Then God gave them King David, a man after God's own heart. David conquered Israel's foes and left a rich, powerful kingdom to his son Solomon.

In spite of all this goodness, throughout their seven hundred-year history, the Israelites repeatedly forsook the Lord and worshiped idols. Finally, God sent them into captivity in Assyria and Babylon. Yet even then the Lord allowed a remnant to return to the land of promise. And then what happened? This group repaid God's goodness by intermarrying with the heathen! With the history of their nation fresh in their minds and with a painful awareness of their own wrongdoing, the people now confessed their sins.

The people confess their present sins

[32]"Now therefore, O our God, the great, mighty and awesome God, who keeps his covenant of love, do not let all this hardship seem trifling in your eyes—the hardship that has come upon us, upon our kings and leaders, upon our priests and prophets, upon our fathers and all your people, from the days of the kings of Assyria until today. [33]In all that has happened to us, you have been just; you have acted faithfully, while we did wrong. [34]Our kings, our leaders, our priests and our fathers did not follow your law; they did not pay attention to your commands or the warnings you gave them. [35]Even while they were in their kingdom, enjoying your great goodness to them in the spacious and fertile land you gave them, they did not serve you or turn from their evil ways.

[36]"But you see, we are slaves today, slaves in the land you gave our forefathers so they could eat its fruit and the other good things it produces. [37]Because of our sins, its abundant harvest goes to the kings you have placed over us. They rule over our bodies and our cattle as they please. We are in great distress.

[38]"In view of all this, we are making a binding agreement, putting it in writing, and our leaders, our Levites and our priests are affixing their seals to it."

The people expressed the same solidarity with previous generations that was typical of the book of Ezra. They admitted that their nation had deserved all the hardships it had suffered, even captivity in Assyria and Babylon. Even though the Persian kings had given them greater freedom, the Jews still felt that their subjection to foreign rulers was a heavy burden. It is a reflection of Ezra's tact and his respect for his king that the rulers of Persia are not named in these negative comments about the rule of foreigners. Although Israel's suffering had been deserved, the people were hopeful that the Lord would grant them further relief.

The Israelites desired to renew the nation's promise to observe God's law. This commitment they now intended to express publicly, formally, and in writing.

The list of those making the covenant

10 Those who sealed it were:
Nehemiah, the governor, son of Hacaliah.

Zedekiah, ²Seraiah, Azariah, Jeremiah, ³Pashhur, Amariah, Malkijah, ⁴Hattush, Sebaniah, Malluch, ⁵Harim, Meremoth, Obadiah, ⁶Daniel, Ginnethon, Baruch, ⁷Meshullam, Abijah, Mijamin, ⁸Maaziah, Bilgai and Shemaiah.
These were the priests.

⁹The Levites:

Jeshua son of Azaniah, Binnui of the sons of Henadad, Kadmiel, ¹⁰and their associates: Shebaniah, Hodiah, Kelita, Pelaiah, Hanan, ¹¹Mica, Rehob, Hashabiah, ¹²Zaccur, Sherebiah, Shebaniah, ¹³Hodiah, Bani and Beninu.

¹⁴The leaders of the people:

Parosh, Pahath-Moab, Elam, Zattu, Bani, ¹⁵Bunni, Azgad, Bebai, ¹⁶Adonijah, Bigvai, Adin, ¹⁷Ater, Hezekiah, Azzur, ¹⁸Hodiah, Hashum, Bezai, ¹⁹Hariph, Anathoth, Nebai, ²⁰Magpiash, Meshullam, Hezir, ²¹Meshezabel, Zadok, Jaddua, ²²Pelatiah, Hanan, Anaiah, ²³Hoshea, Hananiah, Hasshub, ²⁴Hallohesh, Pilha, Shobek, ²⁵Rehum, Hashabnah, Maaseiah, ²⁶Ahiah, Hanan, Anan, ²⁷Malluch, Harim and Baanah.

²⁸**"The rest of the people—priests, Levites, gatekeepers, singers, temple servants and all who separated themselves from the neighboring peoples for the sake of the Law of God, together with their wives and all their sons and daughters who are able to understand—²⁹all these now join their brothers the nobles, and bind themselves with a curse and an oath to follow the Law of God given through Moses the servant of God and to obey carefully all the commands, regulations and decrees of the LORD our Lord.**

In response to the reading of the Law and the admonition of the Levites, the people of Judah promised to obey all the laws and worship regulations the Lord had given to them through Moses. Nehemiah's name stands in a place of honor at the head of the list. It is surprising that Ezra does not receive similar recognition. If this section is based on Ezra's own account of the covenant ceremony, he may have omitted his name out of modesty. It is not clear if the name of Zedekiah should be joined with that of Nehemiah or if it is part of the list of priests that follows. In the original Hebrew the names are joined by an "and." If Zedekiah is supposed to be joined with Nehemiah, as the verse division of our English translations suggests, he was probably Nehemiah's assistant.

Some of the 21 priests listed here have the same names as well-known biblical characters, but they are not the same men. We do not know anything about any of the men in this list, except Nehemiah. Several of the Levites mentioned here were apparently the same men who assisted Ezra in Nehemiah chapter 8. We know nothing about any of these Levites beyond the fact that they were mentioned in these lists. The first part of the list of lay leaders is very similar to the lists in Ezra chapter 2 and Nehemiah chapter 7. It seems likely, therefore, that these were the names of families, rather than individuals. The additional names that do not appear in the earlier lists were probably families or clans that had achieved independent status since the time of Zerubbabel. No doubt many laypeople, who did not sign the document as the leaders did, made the same commitment as their leaders. They too joined in the covenant ceremony.

This list is a memorial to those who pledged their faithfulness to the Lord. Although most of them are unknown and long forgotten, their names still stand in Scripture as a memorial to their faithfulness and to the grace of God, which led them to the stand they took. This list reminds us that when our names and deeds of faith have been forgotten by other people, God will still remember. With the Lord there are no forgotten names.

The terms of the covenant

[30]"We promise not to give our daughters in marriage to the peoples around us or take their daughters for our sons.

[31]"When the neighboring peoples bring merchandise or grain to sell on the Sabbath, we will not buy from them on the Sabbath or on any holy day. Every seventh year we will forgo working the land and will cancel all debts.

[32]"We assume the responsibility for carrying out the commands to give a third of a shekel each year for the service of the house of our God: [33]for the bread set out on the table; for the regular grain offerings and burnt offerings; for the offerings on the Sabbaths, New Moon festivals and appointed feasts; for the holy offerings; for sin offerings to make atonement for Israel; and for all the duties of the house of our God.

[34]"We—the priests, the Levites and the people—have cast lots to determine when each of our families is to bring to the house of our God at set times each year a contribution of wood to burn on the altar of the LORD our God, as it is written in the Law.

³⁵"We also assume responsibility for bringing to the house of the LORD each year the firstfruits of our crops and of every fruit tree.

³⁶"As it is also written in the Law, we will bring the firstborn of our sons and of our cattle, of our herds and of our flocks to the house of our God, to the priests ministering there.

³⁷"Moreover, we will bring to the storerooms of the house of our God, to the priests, the first of our ground meal, of our grain offerings, of the fruit of all our trees and of our new wine and oil. And we will bring a tithe of our crops to the Levites, for it is the Levites who collect the tithes in all the towns where we work. ³⁸A priest descended from Aaron is to accompany the Levites when they receive the tithes, and the Levites are to bring a tenth of the tithes up to the house of our God, to the storerooms of the treasury. ³⁹The people of Israel, including the Levites, are to bring their contributions of grain, new wine and oil to the storerooms where the articles for the sanctuary are kept and where the ministering priests, the gatekeepers and the singers stay.

"We will not neglect the house of our God."

The people promised to observe the regulations God gave to Moses, regulations that we call the civil and ceremonial law. A Bible dictionary, encyclopedia, or commentary on the following passages from Exodus, Leviticus, Numbers, and Deuteronomy will help those who are interested in more information about the regulations.

Intermarriage with the surrounding peoples was one of the most troublesome problems confronting Ezra and Nehemiah. We discussed this problem in the commentary on Ezra chapter 10.

The obligation to observe the weekly Sabbath Day rest is recorded in Exodus 20:8-11. In addition, the Israelites were to give their land a rest by not farming it every seventh year. The regulations for this sabbatical year are found in Leviticus 25:2-7 and Deuteronomy 15:1-3. During this year debtors were to receive a fresh start by having their debts canceled. The observance of these regulations was a special test of faith; the Israelites had to have confidence that the Lord would provide for them even if they did not plant crops in the seventh year. It required a special measure of generosity to cancel the debts that were due them at the very time they were giving up their normal agricultural income!

The rest of the covenant emphasized various offerings for the support of the temple services. The Law required that each male over 20 years of age pay a half-shekel offering as a ransom for his life (Exodus 30:11-16). If the third of a shekel offering was a continuation of that practice, the reduction in the amount could have been due to the people's poverty or to a different monetary system under the Persian Empire.

The "bread set out on the table" refers to the 12 loaves that had to be placed on the table in the Holy Place of the temple each week (Leviticus 24:5-9). The traditional English name for this offering is the "show bread." The regular offerings for various festivals are summarized in Numbers chapters 28 and 29 and other passages in the books of Moses. Leviticus chapters 1 through 7 discuss the various categories of personal offerings.

The firstfruits and the tithes are summarized in Deuteronomy 14:22-29 and 26:1-15. The redemption of firstborn sons and the sacrifice of firstborn animals was commanded in Exodus 13:12,13 and 34:19,20. This redemption commemorated the sparing of the Israelites' firstborn in Egypt. Although Leviticus often mentions the need for wood for the sacrifices, it contained no specific command for bringing wood. This may have been a new obligation that was being assumed for the first time in Nehemiah's day.

Although these particular regulations and obligations no longer apply to us, the principle "we will not neglect the house of our God" remains unchanged. We who have seen the fulfillment of God's promises in Christ have even more reason to support the gospel with our time and possessions. The wholehearted support of these Old Testament believers for the Lord's work encourages us to pledge the same dedication that we see in them.

The Holy City is repopulated

This next section resumes the story begun in Nehemiah 7:4,5. In those passages Nehemiah planned the repopulation of Jerusalem and began the census necessary for such resettlement. Now after the intervening account about the renewal of the covenant, we return to the topic of resettlement.

11 **Now the leaders of the people settled in Jerusalem, and the rest of the people cast lots to bring one out of every ten to live in Jerusalem, the holy city, while the remaining nine were to stay in their own towns. ²The people commended all the men who volunteered to live in Jerusalem.**

Apparently the leaders had already settled in the capital city of Jerusalem. But the newly restored city was still very short of population. Because of Jerusalem's status as the Holy City that God had chosen as the site of his temple, it was inappropriate that it be left in such a neglected state.

The choosing of names by lottery indicates that few people were eager to leave their farms in the surrounding territory to maintain and defend the newly fortified capital. Ten percent of the people were selected to move to Jerusalem; this was a sort of tithe to the Lord. Perhaps those "who volunteered to live in Jerusalem" were volunteers in addition to those chosen by lot. But this verse could also mean that those chosen by lot gladly accepted the decision and regarded the lot as a decision made by God, rather than an arbitrary imposition by Nehemiah.

The rest of this chapter is a collection of lists concerning the repopulation of Jerusalem. It emphasizes the concern of Nehemiah and Ezra that Jerusalem be repopulated by people with a clear Jewish lineage and that the temple be served by priests and Levites with the family heritage that had been prescribed by the Lord.

The lay leaders who lived in Jerusalem

³These are the provincial leaders who settled in Jerusalem (now some Israelites, priests, Levites, temple servants and descendants of Solomon's servants lived in the towns of Judah, each on his own property in the various towns, ⁴while other people from both Judah and Benjamin lived in Jerusalem):

From the descendants of Judah:

Athaiah son of Uzziah, the son of Zechariah, the son of Amariah, the son of Shephatiah, the son of Mahalalel, a descendant of Perez; ⁵and Maaseiah son of Baruch, the son of Col-Hozeh, the son of Hazaiah, the son of Adaiah, the son of Joiarib, the son of Zechariah, a descendant of Shelah. ⁶The descendants of Perez who lived in Jerusalem totaled 468 able men.

⁷From the descendants of Benjamin:

Sallu son of Meshullam, the son of Joed, the son of Pedaiah, the son of Kolaiah, the son of Maaseiah, the son of Ithiel, the son of Jeshaiah, ⁸and his followers, Gabbai and Sallai—928 men. ⁹Joel son of Zicri was their chief officer, and Judah son of Hassenuah was over the Second District of the city.

These lists are very brief summaries. Their purpose was not to list all the settlers, but to establish the credentials of the settlers as people who could establish a clear genealogy as descendants of Israel. Only two leaders—Athaiah and Maaseiah—were named for the tribe of Judah, but their origins were traced back to Perez and Shelah, the sons of Jacob's son Judah (Genesis 46:12). Likewise, only three leaders—Sallu, Gabbai, Sallai—were named for Benjamin. In this case the genealogy is not traced back to the first generation of the tribe of Benjamin, perhaps because of the near destruction this tribe had suffered in its early history (Judges 20,21). The term *followers* is applied to Gabbai and Sallai. The expression literally means "after him" and most likely means after Sallu in the listing.

Joel and Judah may have been leaders of the Benjamites. But it seems more likely that they were lay leaders for the city and not for a particular tribal group. Their names appear after the total number of Benjamites.

The temple workers who settled in Jerusalem

¹⁰From the priests:

Jedaiah; the son of Joiarib; Jakin; ¹¹Seraiah son of Hilkiah, the son of Meshullam, the son of Zadok, the son of Meraioth, the son of Ahitub, supervisor of the house of God, ¹²and their associates, who carried on the work of the temple—822 men; Adaiah son of Jeroham, the son of Pelaliah, the son of Amzi, the son of Zechariah, the son of Pashhur, the son of Malkijah, ¹³and his associates, who were heads of families—242 men; Amashsai son of Azarel, the son of Ahzai, the son of Meshillemoth, the son of Immer, ¹⁴and his associates, who were able men—128. Their chief officer was Zabdiel son of Haggedolim.

¹⁵From the Levites:

Shemaiah son of Hasshub, the son of Azrikam, the son of Hashabiah, the son of Bunni; ¹⁶Shabbethai and Jozabad, two of the heads of the Levites, who had charge of the

outside work of the house of God; ¹⁷Mattaniah son of
Mica, the son of Zabdi, the son of Asaph, the director who
led in thanksgiving and prayer; Bakbukiah, second among
his associates; and Abda son of Shammua, the son of
Galal, the son of Jeduthun. ¹⁸The Levites in the holy city
totaled 284.

¹⁹The gatekeepers:

Akkub, Talmon and their associates, who kept watch at the
gates—172 men.

The list of the priests has a number of difficulties,
which may be the result of some copying errors. The
word *Haggedolim* is not a personal name but a Hebrew
word meaning "the great ones." If this was a man's name,
it was very unusual, especially because it is a plural.
Amashsai is not a Hebrew name but appears to be a mixture of two names. The beginning of the list presents the
most perplexing problem. Perhaps some words have been
lost from the text here. If the words *son of* were supplied
before and after the name Jakin, the section of the list
from Jedaiah to Ahitub would form one connected genealogy. If this were the case, this part of the list would follow
the same pattern as the other lists in this chapter. If the list
from Jedaiah to Ahitub is one connected genealogy, Jedaiah
would be the leader of the priests who moved to
Jerusalem at the time of Nehemiah, and the other people
in the list would all be his ancestors. This seems plausible
since Seraiah was the name of a priest who returned with
Zerubbabel (Nehemiah 12:1) and, being the third name
before Jedaiah, he would be in the right position to be the
same man as the Seraiah who returned with Zerubbabel.
In a parallel list in 1 Chronicles 9:10,11, however, Jedaiah,
Jehoiarib, Jakin, and Azariah do not appear to be steps in
a genealogy. They seem to be contemporaries. If this
interpretation of the list is correct, we have four members

of the high priestly family from Nehemiah's day listed here, rather than one.

The repetition of the same names in different generations of the priestly families makes any solution of this problem uncertain. The name Ahitub, which is the earliest link in this genealogy regardless of whether it begins from Jedaiah or Seraiah, was the name of at least two high priests in the history of Israel (1 Chronicles 6:7-11). The name Ahitub identifies this section of the list as the genealogy of the Kohathite family of priests that supplied the high priests of Israel. There were three main priestly families in Israel. The other two groups in this section, those led by Adaiah and Amashsai, may have represented the other two important priestly families, the Gershonites and Merarites. Numbers chapters 3 and 4 give the background on the three main families of priests.

Perhaps a few words are in order concerning textual or copying errors in our present text of the Bible. This possibility does not deny the inspiration of Scripture, which applies only to the so-called autographs, the original documents of Scripture. Some copying errors have crept into the manuscripts of the Bible during the centuries in which the Bible was copied by hand. None of these errors raises doubt about any teaching of Scripture. Most of these errors can be corrected easily from the context or from other manuscripts of the Bible. The realization that such copying errors exist in our present texts of the Bible is not a new or "liberal" discovery. Back in the 1500s Martin Luther recognized and discussed a number of the copying, or scribal, problems in the Old Testament text. Such copying errors daily occur in long lists of names and numbers. For example, in the first typing of this commentary several names were omitted from some of the lists. Even after careful proofreading there might still be mistakes in the final product. The misprints we find even in the best magazines or newspapers illustrate the difficulties of producing perfect copies, but the mistakes rarely affect the meaning. This is the kind of mistake we are talking about in regard to the Bible; no teaching of Scripture is affected by such errors.

The list of the Levites is unusual in that Levites and singers have been combined into one list, contrary to the normal practice. The "outside work" of the Levites may refer to such work as collecting tithes and offerings. The gatekeepers were the temple gatekeepers. They performed functions similar to those of our ushers, security guards, and custodians of property.

The settlements of the people

²⁰The rest of the Israelites, with the priests and Levites, were in all the towns of Judah, each on his ancestral property.

²¹The temple servants lived on the hill of Ophel, and Ziha and Gishpa were in charge of them.

²²The chief officer of the Levites in Jerusalem was Uzzi son of Bani, the son of Hashabiah, the son of Mattaniah, the son of Mica. Uzzi was one of Asaph's descendants, who were the singers responsible for the service of the house of God. ²³The singers were under the king's orders, which regulated their daily activity.

²⁴Pethahiah son of Meshezabel, one of the descendants of Zerah son of Judah, was the king's agent in all affairs relating to the people.

²⁵As for the villages with their fields, some of the people of Judah lived in Kiriath Arba and its surrounding settlements, in Dibon and its settlements, in Jekabzeel and its villages, ²⁶in Jeshua, in Moladah, in Beth Pelet, ²⁷in Hazar Shual, in Beersheba and its settlements, ²⁸in Ziklag, in Meconah and its settlements, ²⁹in En Rimmon, in Zorah, in Jarmuth, ³⁰Zanoah, Adullam and their villages, in Lachish and its fields, and in Azekah and its settlements. So they were living all the way from Beersheba to the Valley of Hinnom.

³¹**The descendants of the Benjamites from Geba lived in Micmash, Aija, Bethel and its settlements, ³²in Anathoth, Nob and Ananiah, ³³in Hazor, Ramah and Gittaim, ³⁴in Hadid, Zeboim and Neballat, ³⁵in Lod and Ono, and in the Valley of the Craftsmen.**
³⁶**Some of the divisions of the Levites of Judah settled in Benjamin.**

This last section of the list contains miscellaneous observations on the settlements of the people. We might expect the information on the Levitical officers to have been included in the preceding section. Pethahiah (verse 24) apparently was the official representative of the Persian king in his dealings with the Jews. The "king's orders" that regulated the singers may have been delivered through him, unless this phrase refers back to the original orders issued by David when he instituted the temple singing centuries earlier (1 Chronicles 25).

Ophel, the home of the temple servants, was the hill just south of the temple mountain in Jerusalem. The cities listed in the last paragraph were spread throughout Judah from Beersheba in the extreme south to the Hinnom Valley, which is the southern border of Jerusalem. This list shows that the Jews had reestablished themselves throughout all areas of Judea. (See the map entitled "Judah after the return," page 200, for the locations of some of these cities.) The cities of Benjamin lay just north of Jerusalem, between Jerusalem and Samaria. Some of the Levites previously assigned to Judah moved to this territory, apparently because it was short of Levites.

The Levites' role in rebuilding Jerusalem

A review of those who returned

12 **These were the priests and Levites who returned with Zerubbabel son of Shealtiel and with Jeshua:**
Seraiah, Jeremiah, Ezra,

²Amariah, Malluch, Hattush,
³Shecaniah, Rehum, Meremoth,
⁴Iddo, Ginnethon, Abijah,
⁵Mijamin, Moadiah, Bilgah,
⁶Shemaiah, Joiarib, Jedaiah,
⁷Sallu, Amok, Hilkiah and Jedaiah.

These were the leaders of the priests and their associates in the days of Jeshua.

—⁸The Levites were Jeshua, Binnui, Kadmiel, Sherebiah, Judah, and also Mattaniah, who, together with his associates, was in charge of the songs of thanksgiving. ⁹Bakbukiah and Unni, their associates, stood opposite them in the services.

—¹⁰Jeshua was the father of Joiakim, Joiakim the father of Eliashib, Eliashib the father of Joiada, ¹¹Joiada the father of Jonathan, and Jonathan the father of Jaddua.

—¹²In the days of Joiakim, these were the heads of the priestly families:

of Seraiah's family, Meraiah;
of Jeremiah's, Hananiah;
¹³of Ezra's, Meshullam;
of Amariah's, Jehohanan;
¹⁴of Malluch's, Jonathan;
of Shecaniah's, Joseph;
¹⁵of Harim's, Adna;
of Meremoth's, Helkai;
¹⁶of Iddo's, Zechariah;
of Ginnethon's, Meshullam;
¹⁷of Abijah's, Zicri;
of Miniamin's and of Moadiah's, Piltai;
¹⁸of Bilgah's, Shammua;
of Shemaiah's, Jehonathan;
¹⁹of Joiarib's, Mattenai;
of Jedaiah's, Uzzi;
²⁰of Sallu's, Kallai;
of Amok's, Eber;
²¹of Hilkiah's, Hashabiah;
of Jedaiah's, Nethanel.

²²The family heads of the Levites in the days of Eliashib, Joiada, Johanan and Jaddua, as well as those of the priests, were recorded

in the reign of Darius the Persian. ²³The family heads among the descendants of Levi up to the time of Johanan son of Eliashib were recorded in the book of the annals. ²⁴And the leaders of the Levites were Hashabiah, Sherebiah, Jeshua son of Kadmiel, and their associates, who stood opposite them to give praise and thanksgiving, one section responding to the other, as prescribed by David the man of God.

²⁵Mattaniah, Bakbukiah, Obadiah, Meshullam, Talmon and Akkub were gatekeepers who guarded the storerooms at the gates. ²⁶They served in the days of Joiakim son of Jeshua, the son of Jozadak, and in the days of Nehemiah the governor and of Ezra the priest and scribe.

Another list! It's easy for us to become frustrated when we read these lists in Nehemiah, because they do not mean as much to us as they did to Nehemiah and his contemporaries. We do not know these people as flesh and blood human beings. And, removed as we are by centuries, we cannot rediscover the significance of each individual name in these lists. Nevertheless, we can form a pretty good idea of the basic purpose of each list.

The main purpose of this list in Nehemiah chapter 12 seems to be to assure the people that the priests and Levites whom they were following were really descendants of the families God appointed to serve in this capacity. This was important if God's people were to have confidence in the validity of the sacrifices offered on their behalf. A second purpose of the list may be to honor those who played a leading part in the restoration of the nation.

Actually, we have not one list here, but four. We've separated these four lists with dashes in the previous text.

The first list (verses 1-7) names 22 leaders of priestly families at the time of the first return under Zerubbabel and Jeshua, one hundred years earlier. Ezra 2:36-39 lists only four divisions of the priesthood at the time of Zerubbabel. This list of 22 leaders may reflect a redivision of the priesthood that comes closer to the 24 orders established by David in 1 Chronicles 24:7-19.

The second list (verses 8,9), the Levitical leaders, is also more extensive than the corresponding list in Ezra chapter 2.

The third list (verses 10,11) gives the line of high priests from the time of Zerubbabel until the writing of the book of Nehemiah. It thus extends the lists of high priests in 1 Chronicles 6:3-15, which go from the time of Moses and Aaron until the exile. Jeshua was priest at the time of the first return under Zerubbabel. Eliashib was priest during the administration of Nehemiah. The list extends three generations past Eliashib, but this does not mean that the list comes from many years after the time of Nehemiah, as critics claim. Eliashib's grandson Jonathan was already a married man in the last years of Nehemiah's administration. The list could easily have been written during Nehemiah's retirement years, very soon after the last events reported in Nehemiah. Jaddua, Eliashib's great-grandson, need not have been high priest at this time. He may merely have been heir to the position.

The fourth list (verses 12-21) summarizes the leadership of the priestly families at the time of Joiakim, just before the reforms of Ezra and Nehemiah. This arrangement probably continued pretty much unchanged during the time of Ezra and Nehemiah. There are only 20 names in this list, as compared with 22 at the time of Zerubbabel (verses 1-7). This indicates that the number of priestly families fluctuated somewhat from one generation to the next.

The concluding paragraph (verses 22-26) gives us some interesting information about one of the sources of the lists in Nehemiah. Important genealogical information about the priests and Levites was gathered into record books for future use. Apparently this took place during the reign of Darius II (423–404 B.C.), shortly after the last events described in Nehemiah. Nehemiah probably used such a record book as a source for his lists.

Nehemiah's catalog of priests demonstrates the preservation of the line of priests. Piecing together the various scriptural lists, we can trace the priesthood, which began with Aaron, over a thousand year period, roughly 140–400 B.C. This shows how carefully God preserved his chosen nation and its institutions. The priesthood was to reach its greatest glory in Christ. He would offer the supreme sacrifice—his spotless life for the sins of the world.

The Levites' role in the dedication of the walls

27At the dedication of the wall of Jerusalem, the Levites were sought out from where they lived and were brought to Jerusalem to celebrate joyfully the dedication with songs of thanksgiving and with the music of cymbals, harps and lyres. 28The singers also were brought together from the region around Jerusalem—from the villages of the Netophathites, 29from Beth Gilgal, and from the area of Geba and Azmaveth, for the singers had built villages for themselves around Jerusalem. 30When the priests and Levites had purified themselves ceremonially, they purified the people, the gates and the wall.

31I had the leaders of Judah go up on top of the wall. I also assigned two large choirs to give thanks. One was to proceed on top of the wall to the right, toward the Dung Gate. 32Hoshaiah and half the leaders of Judah followed them, 33along with Azariah, Ezra, Meshullam, 34Judah, Benjamin, Shemaiah, Jeremiah, 35as well as some priests with trumpets, and also Zechariah son of Jonathan, the son of Shemaiah, the son of Mattaniah, the son of Micaiah, the son of Zaccur, the son of Asaph, 36and his associates—Shemaiah, Azarel, Milalai, Gilalai, Maai, Nethanel, Judah

and Hanani—with musical instruments prescribed by David the man of God. Ezra the scribe led the procession. ³⁷At the Fountain Gate they continued directly up the steps of the City of David on the ascent to the wall and passed above the house of David to the Water Gate on the east.

³⁸The second choir proceeded in the opposite direction. I followed them on top of the wall, together with half the people—past the Tower of the Ovens to the Broad Wall, ³⁹over the Gate of Ephraim, the Jeshanah Gate, the Fish Gate, the Tower of Hananel and the Tower of the Hundred, as far as the Sheep Gate. At the Gate of the Guard they stopped.

⁴⁰The two choirs that gave thanks then took their places in the house of God; so did I, together with half the officials, ⁴¹as well as the priests—Eliakim, Maaseiah, Miniamin, Micaiah, Elioenai, Zechariah and Hananiah with their trumpets—⁴²and also Maaseiah, Shemaiah, Eleazar, Uzzi, Jehohanan, Malkijah, Elam and Ezer. The choirs sang under the direction of Jezrahiah. ⁴³And on that day they offered great sacrifices, rejoicing because God had given them great joy. The women and children also rejoiced. The sound of rejoicing in Jerusalem could be heard far away.

⁴⁴At that time men were appointed to be in charge of the storerooms for the contributions, firstfruits and tithes. From the fields around the towns they were to bring into the storerooms the portions required by the Law for the priests and the Levites, for Judah was pleased with the ministering priests and Levites. ⁴⁵They performed the service of their God and the service of purification, as did also the singers and gatekeepers, according to the commands of David and his son Solomon. ⁴⁶For long ago, in the days of David and Asaph, there had been directors for the singers and for the songs of praise and thanksgiving to God. ⁴⁷So in the days of Zerubbabel and of Nehemiah, all Israel contributed the daily portions for the singers and gatekeepers. They also set aside the portion for the other Levites, and the Levites set aside the portion for the descendants of Aaron.

The dedication of the walls apparently took place shortly after the completion of the walls and the repopulation of Jerusalem described in Nehemiah chapters 6 and 7—that is,

Procession on the walls of Jerusalem

about 444 B.C. The "I" in the text indicates that this part of the book is based on Nehemiah's own memories of the event.

The celebration began somewhere on the western wall of the city, probably at the Valley Gate. Ezra led one choir and procession counterclockwise around the city along the west, south, and east walls of the city. Nehemiah accompanied the other choir in procession clockwise along the west and north walls of the city. The two groups met at the temple in the northeast corner of the city for the special dedication service. (See the map entitled "Nehemiah's Jerusalem," page 201, to review the location of some of the city landmarks.) The celebrants had "purified" themselves. Such ceremonial cleansing could include fasting, washing, and abstention from sex (Exodus 19:10-15; 1 Samuel 7:6). The sacrifices and music added to this special occasion. The joy of having Jerusalem restored at last made the dedication ceremony a day to be long remembered.

The enthusiasm generated by the celebration spilled over. The people gladly increased their support for the temple, and the priests and Levites carried out their duties with a renewed diligence. Both the people and the priests were conscious of carrying on the traditions established in Israel's glory days during the reigns of David and Solomon. Asaph was music director under David and Solomon; a dozen psalms are attributed to him.

Now it seemed that Israel was entering a new golden age, at least in spiritual strength. But the next chapter shows that the bright happiness of this day soon faded away.

Nehemiah's final reforms

Nehemiah purifies the temple

13 On that day the Book of Moses was read aloud in the hearing of the people and there it was found written that no Ammonite or Moabite should ever be admitted into the assembly of God, ²because they had not met the Israelites with food and water but had hired Balaam to call a curse down on them. (Our God, however, turned the curse into a blessing.) ³When the people heard this law, they excluded from Israel all who were of foreign descent.

⁴Before this Eliashib the priest had been put in charge of the storerooms of the house of our God. He was closely associated with Tobiah, ⁵and he had provided him with a large room formerly used to store the grain offerings and incense and temple articles, and also the tithes of grain, new wine and oil prescribed for the Levites, singers and gatekeepers, as well as the contributions for the priests.

⁶But while all this was going on, I was not in Jerusalem, for in the thirty-second year of Artaxerxes king of Babylon I had returned to the king. Some time later I asked his permission ⁷and came back to Jerusalem. Here I learned about the evil thing Eliashib had done in providing Tobiah a room in the courts of the house of God. ⁸I was greatly displeased and threw all Tobiah's household goods out of the room. ⁹I gave orders to purify the rooms, and then I put back into them the equipment of the house of God, with the grain offerings and the incense.

¹⁰I also learned that the portions assigned to the Levites had not been given to them, and that all the Levites and singers responsible for the service had gone back to their own fields. ¹¹So I rebuked the officials and asked them, "Why is the house of God neglected?" Then I called them together and stationed them at their posts.

¹²All Judah brought the tithes of grain, new wine and oil into the storerooms. ¹³I put Shelemiah the priest, Zadok the scribe, and a Levite named Pedaiah in charge of the storerooms and made Hanan son of Zaccur, the son of Mattaniah, their assistant, because these men were considered trustworthy. They were made responsible for distributing the supplies to their brothers.

¹⁴Remember me for this, O my God, and do not blot out what I have so faithfully done for the house of my God and its services.

There appears to be an interval of about 15 years between chapters 12 and 13 of Nehemiah. The dedication of the walls (chapter 12) probably took place in about 444 B.C., soon after their completion. Nehemiah returned to Persia in the 32nd year of Artaxerxes, about 433 B.C. Israel's spiritual relapse (chapter 13) took place during Nehemiah's absence from Jerusalem. We are not told how long he was away from Jerusalem, but it was probably a number of years before he returned to carry out the reforms described in chapter 13. These reforms may have taken place as late as 425 B.C. The words "On that day" that begin this section apparently do not refer to the dedication day described in chapter 12. To avoid confusion, they might better be translated "On a certain day."

It is shocking that the people would so quickly break the covenant they had made with the Lord and return to the evil practices that the reforms of Ezra and Nehemiah had corrected. It was doubly shocking that the leading priestly families were among the ringleaders of this apostasy. Shocking as it may be, such rapid apostasy was by no means unprecedented in Israel's history. Remember how quickly the Israelites had broken their covenant at Mount Sinai by their worship of the golden calf (Exodus 32).

Some commentators have suggested that Eliashib the priest, who took Tobiah the Ammonite into the temple, could not have been the same Eliashib who was high priest during Nehemiah's governorship. They argue that the high priest would not be concerned about the routine operations of the temple's storage rooms. Yet it seems most natural to assume that this is indeed the same Eliashib who was high priest. Even if the high priest did not participate directly in the daily management of the storerooms, he undoubtedly was responsible for the overall management of the supplies during Nehemiah's absence.

Nehemiah 13:28 makes it clear that Eliashib's family was guilty of participation in the illegal mixed marriages.

Nehemiah 6:18 says that both Tobiah and his son were married to Jewish women. The web of intermarriages linking the noble families of Judah with Tobiah and Sanballat, the enemies of Israel, was the direct cause of this profaning of the temple.

One might think it was relatively harmless to let Tobiah live in a storage room. But by this move, he was able to set up a base to undo the reforms of Ezra and Nehemiah in the very heart of the temple. Furthermore, these were no ordinary storage rooms. They were "holy" because they were set aside for gathering the sacred offerings that were to support the temple ministry. While the rooms were being used by the enemy of Israel, the gathering of the offerings was neglected and the temple workers were forced to abandon their ministries and go to the country to eke out a living in farming. Compromise and accommodation with the enemies of God's Word are never harmless, but ultimately undermine and destroy the work of God's people.

The first step toward correcting this tragic situation again came through a return to God's Word. Through the words of Scripture, the people were reminded that Israel's enemies, the Moabites and Ammonites, were not to be included in the religious life of Israel (Deuteronomy 23:3-6). During Israel's wandering in the wilderness, these enemies had hired Balaam, a prophet, to curse the Israelites. Following the famous incident in which Balaam's donkey miraculously spoke to him, Balaam blessed the Israelites instead of cursing them (Numbers 22–24).

Upon his return to Jerusalem, Nehemiah resorted to strong measures in order to restore the reforms he and Ezra had previously put into effect. Tobiah was forcibly ejected from the temple. The system for supporting the temple workers was reestablished. The leaders were sharply rebuked for their negligence. Nehemiah closed this section with a brief prayer that God would remember his faithfulness and that the reforms he had established would not be overthrown.

Nehemiah honors the Sabbath

¹⁵In those days I saw men in Judah treading winepresses on the Sabbath and bringing in grain and loading it on donkeys, together with wine, grapes, figs and all other kinds of loads. And they were bringing all this into Jerusalem on the Sabbath. Therefore I warned them against selling food on that day. ¹⁶Men from Tyre who lived in Jerusalem were bringing in fish and all kinds of merchandise and selling them in Jerusalem on the Sabbath to the people of Judah. ¹⁷I rebuked the nobles of Judah and said to them, "What is this wicked thing you are doing—desecrating the Sabbath day? ¹⁸Didn't your forefathers do the same things so that our God brought all this calamity upon us and upon this city? Now you are stirring up more wrath against Israel by desecrating the Sabbath."

¹⁹When evening shadows fell on the gates of Jerusalem before the Sabbath, I ordered the doors to be shut and not opened until the Sabbath was over. I stationed some of my own men at the gates so that no load could be brought in on the Sabbath day. ²⁰Once or twice the merchants and sellers of all kinds of goods spent the night outside Jerusalem. ²¹But I warned them and said, "Why do you spend the night by the wall? If you do this again, I will lay hands on you." From that time on they no longer came on the Sabbath. ²²Then I commanded the Levites to purify themselves and go and guard the gates in order to keep the Sabbath day holy.

Remember me for this also, O my God, and show mercy to me according to your great love.

The violation of the Sabbath was especially shocking because it set aside one of the most basic commandments of God. How quickly the Jews were becoming just like their neighbors! Soon they would have blended invisibly into their heathen surroundings. Nehemiah again took strong action to restore the proper observance of the Sabbath. He reminded the people that violation of the Sabbath had been one of the basic causes of Jerusalem's destruction, as the people had ignored God's warnings through the prophet Jeremiah: "If you do not obey me to keep the Sabbath day holy by not carrying any load as you come through the gates of Jerusalem on the Sabbath day, then I will kindle an unquenchable fire in the gates of Jerusalem that will consume her fortresses" (Jeremiah 17:27).

When admonition was not enough to do the job, Nehemiah used his police power as governor. He forcibly put an end to the merchandising on the Sabbath, especially that of the Phoenician traders from Tyre. Again Nehemiah prayed that the Lord would not forget his faithful efforts to reform the nation.

Nehemiah opposes intermarriage

²³Moreover, in those days I saw men of Judah who had married women from Ashdod, Ammon and Moab. ²⁴Half of their children spoke the language of Ashdod or the language of one of the other peoples, and did not know how to speak the language of Judah. ²⁵I rebuked them and called curses down on them. I beat some of the men and pulled out their hair. I made them take an oath in God's name and said: "You are not to give your daughters in marriage to their sons, nor are you to take their daughters in marriage for your sons or for yourselves. ²⁶Was it not because of marriages like these that Solomon king of Israel sinned? Among the many nations there was no king like him. He was loved by his God, and God made him king over all Israel, but even he was led into sin by foreign women. ²⁷Must we hear now that you too are doing all this terrible wickedness and are being unfaithful to our God by marrying foreign women?"

²⁸One of the sons of Joiada son of Eliashib the high priest was son-in-law to Sanballat the Horonite. And I drove him away from me.

²⁹Remember them, O my God, because they defiled the priestly office and the covenant of the priesthood and of the Levites.

30So I purified the priests and the Levites of everything foreign, and assigned them duties, each to his own task. 31I also made provision for contributions of wood at designated times, and for the firstfruits.

Remember me with favor, O my God.

One of Ezra's most basic reforms had been his action against illegal intermarriages with heathen neighbors (Ezra 10). The people had renewed their pledge to avoid these forbidden marriages during the governorship of Nehemiah: "We promise not to give our daughters in marriage to the peoples around us or take their daughters for our sons" (Nehemiah 10:30). Nevertheless, as soon as Nehemiah left Jerusalem, they quickly returned to this practice. Since Ezra is not mentioned in this chapter, it may be that he too was no longer on the scene. Perhaps the work of the prophet Malachi, who opposed these intermarriages and the neglect of the temple offerings, took place during Nehemiah's absence (Malachi 2,3).

Again it is shocking to note that the spiritual leaders of Israel, including the family of the high priest, were among the chief offenders in this matter. One of the bad effects of these intermarriages on the religious life of Israel was the loss of the Hebrew language, the language of Scripture, as the Jews turned more and more to the dialects of their neighbors.

Once again Nehemiah took drastic action to curb the abuses. He reminded the people of the devastating consequences of such intermarriages in the past history of Israel, especially those intermarriages that took place during the life of Solomon (1 Kings 11:1-10). Nehemiah expelled the unfaithful priest from his position in the temple and took harsh action against others guilty of such marriages. The plucking of the hair or beard seems to have been a humiliating punishment (Isaiah 50:6; 2 Samuel 10:4). Again

Nehemiah prayed, this time that the Lord would not forget the unfaithfulness of those who defiled the holy office of the priesthood, but that they would get the punishment they deserved.

The closing sentences serve as a memorial to all the work of Nehemiah. It is significant that Nehemiah made no mention of his great work of restoring the walls of Jerusalem. He wished to be remembered most for his contributions to the spiritual reform of Israel. Though he was a layman, it was his spiritual work that meant the most to him, rather than his achievements as governor of the nation.

The book of Nehemiah remains a memorial to the vital role this dedicated layman played at a crucial point in the history of Israel. Side by side, Ezra the priest and Nehemiah the governor labored faithfully to guide the people of Israel, so that at least a remnant would remain faithful to the Lord until the Messiah appeared. The book of Nehemiah also stands as a testimony to the faithfulness of the Lord. Throughout history God provides his people with strong leaders at critical times, so that the gospel may be preserved among them until he returns.

INTRODUCTION TO ESTHER

Background

The events described in the book of Esther took place between the sixth and seventh chapters of Ezra, after the return of Zerubbabel but before the return of Ezra. In this book we learn how God used Esther to save the people of Israel from destruction. Through Esther, God preserved the tiny remnant in Judah that had rebuilt the temple under the leadership of Zerubbabel and Jeshua. The Jews who were still scattered in Babylonia and other parts of the Persian Empire were also preserved so that some of them could participate in the returns led by Ezra and Nehemiah. In this way God kept a faithful remnant of his people and established some of them in the Promised Land. There they would await the long-promised Messiah.

We do not know who wrote the book of Esther. Mordecai, one of the main characters in the book, has been suggested as the author, but Esther 10:2,3 seems to indicate that someone else was the author. Since the book refers to records kept in the Persian court, it may have been written by Ezra, Nehemiah, or some other Jew employed by the Persian court.

Some theologians have suggested that Esther should not be included in the canon of the Old Testament but should be placed among the Apocrypha. (The canon is the list of books that the church recognizes as the inspired Word of God. The Apocrypha are religious books written by the Jews in the years between the Old and New Testaments. They make for interesting reading, but they are not inspired

Scripture.) Esther therefore does not belong among the books of the Bible called *homologoumena* (the books accepted by everyone at all times), but among those called *antilegomena* (those that some people have spoken against). Both Jewish and Christian theologians have raised questions about the canonicity of Esther. Luther was among those who have made derogatory remarks about Esther, but his observations about the book were offhand comments, rather than a thorough evaluation. We must remember that Luther realized that Roman Catholicism had accepted some apocryphal books into the Old Testament, and there were reasons to ask if Esther might be one of them.

The most serious objection to including Esther among the Old Testament books is the complete absence of the name of God from the book. The book does not specifically mention prayer or any important feature of Old Testament worship except fasting. The piety that is so obvious in Ezra and Nehemiah is almost totally absent from Esther. The Septuagint, the Greek translation of the Old Testament widely used in the early Christian church, added a number of passages to Esther in order to make the book "more religious"; it introduced the name of God and prayer. These additions can be found in a Roman Catholic edition of the Bible, such as the Jerusalem Bible, and in most editions of the Apocrypha.

Rather than helping, these additions have only increased suspicion of the book. The book is not quoted or referred to in the New Testament. Nor does it appear among the Dead Sea Scrolls, the most important find of ancient Old Testament manuscripts. For Jews an additional reason for questioning Esther was that it adds Purim, a new festival, to the festivals that God gave to Moses at Mount Sinai. Since the Purim celebration often involves wild celebrating and drinking, some Jews have had doubts about Esther. Many

Jews are also offended by the vengeful spirit that the Jews seem to exhibit in the latter part of the book. If the book was written in Persia, it may not have become well known in Israel for some time after it was written. Such a delayed acceptance would be especially likely if Esther was written after Ezra and Nehemiah had left Babylon. All of these factors contributed to the uncertainty that some Christians and Jews have felt about the book of Esther.

In spite of all this, there is no compelling reason to doubt the authenticity of the book of Esther. Its position in the canon of the Old Testament is well established. A knowledge of Esther is also apparent in the Apocrypha and in the writings of Josephus, the famous Jewish historian of the first century. Obviously the ancient Jews knew and made use of the book of Esther. Most of the book's peculiarities can be explained by the fact that it is written in the style of a Persian narrative. The book is deliberately written in a secular style to reflect the point of view of a person living outside of the Holy Land in an unholy heathen kingdom. This secular style of the book may account for the near absence of religious elements from the work. It may also be that Mordecai and Esther were not particularly religious in their daily lives. Unlike Daniel and his friends, Esther may have hidden her faith. God is certainly not limited to using models of personal piety to accomplish his purposes. It is possible that the lack of piety in the book is an accurate reflection of the lifestyle of Esther, who had conformed to the Persian way of life. The absence of God's name and the lack of piety in the book are actually strong evidence for the authenticity of the book. If the book were written by a pious Jew in Palestine long after the time of Esther, he would probably have included references to piety and observance of the Law, exactly as the Septuagint translator did when he made his additions. The secular tone of the book reflects the conditions and attitudes of Jews scattered in Persia, rather than those of pious Jews in the Holy Land.

Additional arguments for the authenticity of Esther are its accurate knowledge of Persian customs and its use of many Persian words. Examples of this will be noted at various points in the commentary.

The lack of personal piety of Esther and Mordecai actually strengthens the value of the book of Esther as a special demonstration of the providence of God. Ezra and Nehemiah were very conscious of being used as the Lord's instruments for the welfare of his people. Esther may have been much less conscious of her role in God's plan. God's will was accomplished just as surely in both cases.

The hand of God is clearly present in the book of Esther, shaping and directing the course of events so that his people would be protected. The hand of God was there even if Esther herself didn't always see it. The book of Esther is especially meaningful for Christians today because, more than any other book of Scripture, it demonstrates the way God works among us at any given time in history. Like Esther, we do not see God's power on display in mighty miracles such as those performed by Moses in Egypt. Today God normally works with the same quiet power that is on display in the book of Esther. But the power and the effect are the same, whether God destroys the enemies of his people with dramatic displays of power as he did in Egypt or turns the hearts of kings with quiet power visible only to the eyes of faith.

In every time and place, God works to protect his people, regardless of the methods he may use. As we read the book of Esther and see how the Lord of history protected his people, let's remember that the same God is still at work.

He guards us and directs this world's history so that all things work "for the good of those who love him" (Romans 8:28).

Outline

    I. The plot against the Jews (1:1–4:17)
      A. Historical setting (1:1–2:23)
      B. The plot of Haman (3:1–4:17)

    II. The delivery of the Jews (5:1–10:3)
      A. Esther's plan (5:1-14)
      B. The rise of Mordecai and downfall of Haman (6:1–7:10)
      C. The triumph of the Jews (8:1–9:32)
      D. The greatness of Mordecai (10:1-3)

PART ONE

The Plot against the Jews
(1:1–4:17)

Historical setting

The royal banquet

1 This is what happened during the time of Xerxes, the Xerxes who ruled over 127 provinces stretching from India to Cush: ²At that time King Xerxes reigned from his royal throne in the citadel of Susa, ³and in the third year of his reign he gave a banquet for all his nobles and officials. The military leaders of Persia and Media, the princes, and the nobles of the provinces were present.

⁴For a full 180 days he displayed the vast wealth of his kingdom and the splendor and glory of his majesty. ⁵When these days were over, the king gave a banquet, lasting seven days, in the enclosed garden of the king's palace, for all the people from the least to the greatest, who were in the citadel of Susa. ⁶The garden had hangings of white and blue linen, fastened with cords of white linen and purple material to silver rings on marble pillars. There were couches of gold and silver on a mosaic pavement of porphyry, marble, mother-of-pearl and other costly stones. ⁷Wine was served in goblets of gold, each one different from the other, and the royal wine was abundant, in keeping with the king's liberality. ⁸By the king's command each guest was allowed to drink in his own way, for the king instructed all the wine stewards to serve each man what he wished.

⁹Queen Vashti also gave a banquet for the women in the royal palace of King Xerxes.

This section skillfully sets the scene for the story of Esther. The writer gives us a colorful picture of the fabulous wealth and power of Esther's future husband, Xerxes, as well as a glimpse of his erratic, tempestuous character.

These characteristics are prominent throughout the book of Esther and agree with the portrait of Xerxes that we have from other historical sources.

The Hebrew name of the king is Achashvayrosh (also spelled Ahasuerus in English), but the NIV uses the Greek form of his name, Xerxes, since this is the form of his name that is well known through secular history. Although a few commentators identify him with a later king of Persia who came after the time of Ezra and Nehemiah, it is very likely that he was Xerxes I (485–465 B.C.). Xerxes I ruled Persia between Darius I, who was king when Zerubbabel rebuilt the temple, and Artaxerxes I, the king during the time of Ezra and Nehemiah. This Xerxes is mentioned in Ezra 4:6. His great power and wealth are clearly pictured in our text. His empire was the largest the world had known up to his time. It stretched from northwest India on the east to northern Greece on the west. It extended through Egypt to Ethiopia (Cush) in the south. Some critics have made a great deal of the fact that Greek historians say the Persian empire was divided into about 30 districts, called satrapies, while the biblical accounts report about 120 provinces. Such critics, however, have created a problem where none exists, since it is likely that "provinces" here refers to smaller subdivisions of the larger satrapies. For example, Judah seems to have been a "province" of the large Trans-Euphrates satrapy.

Xerxes is well known to students of ancient history because of his prominent role in Greek history. His father, Darius, had failed in his attempt to conquer Greece when his invading Persian forces were defeated by the Greeks at the famous battle of Marathon in 490 B.C. Xerxes was determined to avenge this defeat and put an end to Greek meddling in the affairs of his empire in Asia Minor (Turkey). In 480 B.C., Xerxes made another invasion against Greece with the largest army and navy ever assembled. Nevertheless, this invasion failed when Xerxes' navy was defeated at Salamis and his land forces were defeated the next year at Platea. This is considered to be one of the most crucial campaigns in the history of the world, since the Greek victory preserved the independence of Greece, the nation whose culture made such great contributions to Western civilization.

A detailed report of this campaign and of the character of Xerxes is preserved in the accounts of the Persian Wars by the Greek historian Herodotus. His description of King Xerxes agrees well with the description in Esther. Herodotus portrays Xerxes as a vain, temperamental ruler and gives many examples of his hot-headed, irrational actions. When the great pontoon bridge that Xerxes had built for his army to cross over into Europe was destroyed by a storm, Xerxes not only executed the bridge builders but also ordered that the sea be whipped and chained for the offense of destroying his bridge! When one of his subjects asked to keep one of his five sons at home while the other four went along with Xerxes to Greece, Xerxes flew into a rage, cut the son into two pieces, laid half his body on each side of the road, and told the father, "There, now you can keep your son at home." We shall see similar impetuous acts of Xerxes in the book of Esther.

Herodotus reports that it took Xerxes four years to prepare for his invasion of Greece, and that he called an assembly of all his nobles to discuss plans for the invasion. It may well be that the great assembly described in Esther chapter 1 was the same as the planning meetings for the invasion of Greece mentioned by Herodotus. Herodotus' stories about Xerxes are very interesting; they are the strongest concurrence between biblical history and secular history that has yet been discovered. Herodotus' portrait of Xerxes offers an interesting parallel with Xerxes' behavior in the following sections of Esther.

Queen Vashti deposed

¹⁰On the seventh day, when King Xerxes was in high spirits from wine, he commanded the seven eunuchs who served him—Mehuman, Biztha, Harbona, Bigtha, Abagtha, Zethar and Carcas—¹¹to bring before him Queen Vashti wearing her royal crown, in order to display her beauty to the people and nobles, for she was lovely to look at. ¹²But when the attendants delivered the king's command, Queen Vashti refused to come. Then the king became furious and burned with anger.

¹³Since it was customary for the king to consult experts in matters of law and justice, he spoke with the wise men who understood the times ¹⁴and were closest to the king—Carshena, Shethar, Admatha, Tarshish, Meres, Marsena and Memucan, the seven nobles of Persia and Media who had special access to the king and were highest in the kingdom.

¹⁵"According to law, what must be done to Queen Vashti?" he asked. "She has not obeyed the command of King Xerxes that the eunuchs have taken to her."

¹⁶Then Memucan replied in the presence of the king and the nobles, "Queen Vashti has done wrong, not only against the king but also against all the nobles and the peoples of all the provinces of King Xerxes. ¹⁷For the queen's conduct will become known to all the women, and so they will despise their husbands and say, 'King Xerxes commanded Queen Vashti to be brought before him, but she would not come.' ¹⁸This very day the Persian and Median women of the nobility who have heard about the queen's conduct will respond to all the king's nobles in the same way. There will be no end of disrespect and discord.

¹⁹"Therefore, if it pleases the king, let him issue a royal decree and let it be written in the laws of Persia and Media, which cannot be repealed, that Vashti is never again to enter the presence of King Xerxes. Also let the king give her royal position to someone else who is better than she. ²⁰Then when the king's edict is proclaimed throughout all his vast realm, all the women will respect their husbands, from the least to the greatest!"

²¹The king and his nobles were pleased with this advice, so the king did as Memucan proposed. ²²He sent dispatches to all parts of

the kingdom, to each province in its own script and to each people in its own language, proclaiming in each people's tongue that every man should be ruler over his own household.

The importance of the story of the removal of Queen Vashti is limited to the fact that it shows how God controlled events so that Esther could become Xerxes' wife. We should be cautious about drawing moral examples from it. Some commentators have made Vashti the hero of the story. They have suggested that since she was ordered to appear wearing the royal crown, she was to appear wearing only the crown, and that she was a noble woman who courageously refused the indecent command of her drunken husband. Others have made Vashti a villain, a disrespectful, arrogant wife who had no regard for her husband. Xerxes' actions seem to be motivated more by pride and anger than by any real understanding or concern for the proper relationship of husband and wife.

It is unlikely that the writer of Esther intended to use either Xerxes or Vashti as a model of moral virtue. He is simply telling how God prepared the way for Esther to become queen. This chapter reminds us that we should be careful not to conclude that every time the Bible *describes* people's actions, it *prescribes* that we should follow their examples. The real lesson in this chapter is not found in the behavior of Xerxes or Vashti but in the power of God, who was invisibly directing human affairs for the ultimate good of his people.

Critics have sometimes claimed that the ridiculous behavior of Xerxes in sending a decree all over the empire just because of one action of his wife is evidence of the fictional nature of the book of Esther. But men have certainly done more ridiculous things than this in the aftermath of a drinking party. The picture of Xerxes in this chapter—

162

drunk, defied, and short tempered—is hardly a flattering one. Yet this portrait of a man rich in power and wealth but poor in judgment and common sense corresponds very well with the picture given by Herodotus. Whether Xerxes was drunk or sober, it is not too hard to imagine that a man who would order the sea whipped because it had offended him would send a letter all over the empire because his wife insulted him in public.

Esther becomes queen

2 Later when the anger of King Xerxes had subsided, he remembered Vashti and what she had done and what he had decreed about her. ²Then the king's personal attendants proposed, "Let a search be made for beautiful young virgins for the king. ³Let the king appoint commissioners in every province of his realm to bring all these beautiful girls into the harem at the citadel of Susa. Let them be placed under the care of Hegai, the king's eunuch, who is in charge of the women; and let beauty treatments be given to them. ⁴Then let the girl who pleases the king be queen instead of Vashti." This advice appealed to the king, and he followed it.

⁵Now there was in the citadel of Susa a Jew of the tribe of Benjamin, named Mordecai son of Jair, the son of Shimei, the son of Kish, ⁶who had been carried into exile from Jerusalem by Nebuchadnezzar king of Babylon, among those taken captive with Jehoiachin king of Judah. ⁷Mordecai had a cousin named Hadassah, whom he had brought up because she had neither father nor mother. This girl, who was also known as Esther, was lovely in form and features, and Mordecai had taken her as his own daughter when her father and mother died.

⁸When the king's order and edict had been proclaimed, many girls were brought to the citadel of Susa and put under the care of Hegai. Esther also was taken to the king's palace and entrusted to Hegai, who had charge of the harem. ⁹The girl pleased him and won his favor. Immediately he provided her with her beauty treatments and special food. He assigned to her seven maids selected

from the king's palace and moved her and her maids into the best place in the harem.

¹⁰Esther had not revealed her nationality and family background, because Mordecai had forbidden her to do so. ¹¹Every day he walked back and forth near the courtyard of the harem to find out how Esther was and what was happening to her.

¹²Before a girl's turn came to go in to King Xerxes, she had to complete twelve months of beauty treatments prescribed for the women, six months with oil of myrrh and six with perfumes and cosmetics. ¹³And this is how she would go to the king: Anything she wanted was given her to take with her from the harem to the king's palace. ¹⁴In the evening she would go there and in the morning return to another part of the harem to the care of Shaashgaz, the king's eunuch who was in charge of the concubines. She would not return to the king unless he was pleased with her and summoned her by name.

¹⁵When the turn came for Esther (the girl Mordecai had adopted, the daughter of his uncle Abihail) to go to the king, she asked for nothing other than what Hegai, the king's eunuch who was in charge of the harem, suggested. And Esther won the favor of everyone who saw her. ¹⁶She was taken to King Xerxes in the royal residence in the tenth month, the month of Tebeth, in the seventh year of his reign.

¹⁷Now the king was attracted to Esther more than to any of the other women, and she won his favor and approval more than any of the other virgins. So he set a royal crown on her head and made her queen instead of Vashti. ¹⁸And the king gave a great banquet, Esther's banquet, for all his nobles and officials. He proclaimed a holiday throughout the provinces and distributed gifts with royal liberality.

This section describes the long process by which Esther became queen of Persia. Four years passed between the decree deposing Vashti and the elevation of Esther. Xerxes' absence during the invasion of Greece may be part of the reason for this delay. The year in which Esther became queen, the seventh year of Xerxes' reign, was 479 B.C., the

Esther presented to the king

year after his defeat at Salamis in Greece. Herodotus reports that Xerxes was accompanied to Greece by a wife named Amestris, who was probably Vashti. She was from a powerful family, and her son Artaxerxes became Xerxes' successor. Xerxes may not have been able to get rid of her as easily as he had hoped. During the trip to Greece, Xerxes attempted to seduce his brother's wife. When this attempt was unsuccessful, he instead had an affair with the woman's daughter, who was married to Xerxes' son. When Amestris found out about this, she avenged herself on this family by horribly mutilating the girl's mother. This action nearly set off a rebellion against Xerxes.

If Vashti and Amestris were indeed the same person, her latest outrage may have been the reason Xerxes pursued the search for a new queen more aggressively after his return from Greece. Another reason for the delay was the long preparation each woman underwent and the probability that Xerxes tried out a large number of candidates for the position. It is impossible to deny the sordid nature of the whole process. Many young virgins were returned to the harem after spending a single night with Xerxes. Many of them apparently never saw him again. The marriage and sexual practices of the Persian court were a far cry from God's intentions when he established marriage, and they also were a far cry from the standards of a pious Jew.

This section also introduces us to Esther and Mordecai, the two main characters in the story. At this time Mordecai was apparently a government official of middle rank in the Persian court. His ancestors had been carried into captivity about 120 years earlier. Kish and Shimei are names that were used in the family of King Saul over five hundred years before the time of Mordecai (1 Samuel 9:1,2; 2 Samuel 16:5); but it appears that these men were Mordecai's immediate ancestors, namesakes of the earlier Kish and Shimei. The phrase "who had been carried into exile" would then describe Kish, who would be Mordecai's great-grandfather. Mordecai's name seems to be a form of the name of the heathen god Marduk. Perhaps the accountant Marduka mentioned in a Persian document is our Mordecai. This practice of having a foreign name was not particularly unusual; even Daniel and his friends had been given second names that incorporated the names of heathen gods (Daniel 1:7). Mordecai's cousin Hadassah, whom he had adopted, had changed her Hebrew name to the name Esther, which appears to be derived from the Persian word for "star," or perhaps from the heathen goddess Ishtar.

Mordecai had a sincere concern and affection for his adopted daughter, so he kept close track of her progress. The text does not give any direct information about the motives of Esther and Mordecai. It is not clear how voluntary Esther's participation was or what role the ambitions of Esther or Mordecai may have played in the matter. Perhaps they had no choice. We are not told. Nevertheless, Esther's willingness to hide her Jewishness would certainly have involved some compromises in her lifestyle and in her worship. In this regard her conduct contrasts sharply with that of Daniel and his three friends (Daniel 1,3).

Esther quickly advanced on the strength of her natural beauty and charm. She gained favor with Hegai, the eunuch in charge of the harem, and relied on his advice concerning what to wear and what to take with her to best please the king when she appeared before him. Hegai undoubtedly knew the king's taste in such matters better than anyone else. In the ancient Near East, the supervisors of the kings' harems were eunuchs, men who had been castrated to remove any possibility that they might engage in sexual relations with one of the king's wives and produce a son who might become heir to the throne. These men were often shrewd politicians who exerted great influence through the women of the court. Hegai's favor for Esther may have been due in part to the fact that he had her picked as a winner and wanted to establish his influence with the future queen. If so, his judgment was sound. She won out and was raised to a position of special prominence among Xerxes' wives. Her rise was celebrated with a special banquet. It is not clear in what sense Esther was "queen" of the Persian empire. She apparently had no sons who could be considered heirs to the throne. In the following chapters it is quite clear that she did not maintain a close husband-wife relationship with Xerxes, and that she had no real role or influence in the affairs of state, except at the whim of Xerxes (Esther 4:11).

Regardless of what the motives of Xerxes, Mordecai, and Esther may have been, God was silently working and directing affairs. At the critical moment, Esther was in a position to play a decisive role in delivering Israel.

Mordecai uncovers a conspiracy

[19]When the virgins were assembled a second time, Mordecai was sitting at the king's gate. [20]But Esther had kept secret her family background and nationality just as Mordecai had told her to do, for she continued to follow Mordecai's instructions as she had done when he was bringing her up.

[21]During the time Mordecai was sitting at the king's gate, Bigthana and Teresh, two of the king's officers who guarded the doorway, became angry and conspired to assassinate King Xerxes. [22]But Mordecai found out about the plot and told Queen Esther, who in turn reported it to the king, giving credit to Mordecai. [23]And when the report was investigated and found to be true, the two officials were hanged on a gallows. All this was recorded in the book of the annals in the presence of the king.

This next development in the story put Mordecai into a position in which the king would owe him a favor at the crucial time in the future when the fate of Israel hung in the balance. Any other details are only incidental to this point.

It is not clear what is meant by the phrase "when the virgins were assembled a second time" or when this event occurred. Mordecai's presence at the palace gate implies he was an official on duty there. The gates of cities and palaces were the sites where much governmental and legal business was carried out. We are told nothing about what motivated two of the king's officials to conspire against his life. It may have been some personal insult or a political conspiracy. Such conspiracies and power struggles were common in the Persian court. In fact, Xerxes ultimately was assassinated as the result of such a conspiracy. The important thing for us to note is how various seemingly unconnected events were all coming together to set up the circumstances in which Israel could be delivered.

The plot of Haman

3 **After these events, King Xerxes honored Haman son of Hammedatha, the Agagite, elevating him and giving him a seat of honor higher than that of all the other nobles. ²All the royal officials at the king's gate knelt down and paid honor to Haman, for the king had commanded this concerning him. But Mordecai would not kneel down or pay him honor.**

³Then the royal officials at the king's gate asked Mordecai, "Why do you disobey the king's command?" ⁴Day after day they spoke to him but he refused to comply. Therefore they told Haman about it to see whether Mordecai's behavior would be tolerated, for he had told them he was a Jew.

⁵When Haman saw that Mordecai would not kneel down or pay him honor, he was enraged. ⁶Yet having learned who Mordecai's people were, he scorned the idea of killing only Mordecai. Instead Haman looked for a way to destroy all Mordecai's people, the Jews, throughout the whole kingdom of Xerxes.

⁷In the twelfth year of King Xerxes, in the first month, the month of Nisan, they cast the *pur* (that is, the lot) in the presence of Haman to select a day and month. And the lot fell on the twelfth month, the month of Adar.

⁸Then Haman said to King Xerxes, "There is a certain people dispersed and scattered among the peoples in all the provinces of your kingdom whose customs are different from those of all other people and who do not obey the king's laws; it is not in the king's best interest to tolerate them. ⁹If it pleases the king, let a decree be issued to destroy them, and I will put ten thousand talents of silver into the royal treasury for the men who carry out this business."

¹⁰So the king took his signet ring from his finger and gave it to Haman son of Hammedatha, the Agagite, the enemy of the Jews. ¹¹"Keep the money," the king said to Haman, "and do with the people as you please."

¹²Then on the thirteenth day of the first month the royal secretaries were summoned. They wrote out in the script of each province and in the language of each people all Haman's orders to the king's satraps, the governors of the various provinces and the nobles of the various peoples. These were written in the name of King Xerxes himself and sealed with his own ring. ¹³Dispatches were sent by couriers to all the king's provinces with the order to destroy, kill and annihilate all the Jews—young and old, women and little children—on a single day, the thirteenth day of the twelfth month, the month of Adar, and to plunder their goods. ¹⁴A copy of the text of the edict was to be issued as law in every province and made known to the people of every nationality so they would be ready for that day.

¹⁵Spurred on by the king's command, the couriers went out, the edict was issued in the citadel of Susa. The king and Haman sat down to drink, but the city of Susa was bewildered.

The remaining events of the book of Esther occur five years after Esther became queen. Haman, the great enemy of God's people, appears abruptly on the scene. We know virtually nothing about his background. According to Jewish tradition, he was a descendant of Agag, king of the Amalekites. The Amalekites were among Israel's most bitter enemies during Israel's early history (Deuteronomy 25:17-19; 1 Samuel 15:8). It seems more likely, however, that Agag here is the name of the region from which Haman came and that the similarity to the name of an ancient Amalekite king is just a coincidence.

Since it was customary for even the highest nobles to bow to the Persian king, it is not surprising that lesser officials were required to give similar honor to the king's highest representative. Mordecai's reasons for refusing to so honor Haman are not entirely clear. There are numerous passages in the Old Testament in which Israelites bowed down to kings or superiors as a sign of respect. For example, Abraham bowed to the Hittite rulers (Genesis 23:7), Jacob's family bowed to Esau (Genesis 33:6), and David bowed to Saul (1 Samuel 24:8). From these examples it is clear that at least in earlier times, it was not considered idolatrous to bow to a human superior. But Mordecai apparently felt that it would be idolatrous to bow down to a heathen ruler, since he justified his action on the grounds that he was a Jew. Perhaps Mordecai's refusal to bow down to any earthly ruler was a reaction against the idolatrous demands that Babylonian and Persian rulers had imposed on Daniel and his friends (Daniel 3,6).

Again, as is so often the case in the book of Esther, the actions of the participants are simply reported without any analysis or moral evaluation of their motives. Nothing in the text indicates whether Mordecai's actions were justified or were a case of misguided zeal. We simply learn how the crisis for the Jewish people came about.

Likewise, we are given little information about the motivation of the officials who reported Mordecai. It appears that they tried to give Mordecai ample time to comply with the king's orders but may finally have felt compelled to report him.

There can be no uncertainty, however, about the attitude and motivation of Haman. He responded with irrational hatred, totally out of proportion to the apparent offense. He

determined to wipe out a whole religion for what he per-
ceived to be the offense of one of its adherents. As shocking
as this is, it should not be particularly surprising. Many more
recent persecutions of both Jews and Christians have been
just as lacking in rational motivation. The tendency of sinful
human beings to hate and fear anyone who is different,
especially anyone whose religious devotion is a silent
rebuke of indifference, is a terrible reality. It has caused a
tremendous amount of pain and bloodshed in this world's
sad history. When the insane rage of Satan against God's
people joins up with this blind human prejudice, reason and
decency are cast aside and hatred runs wild.

But under the wise rule of God's justice, the persecutors
and tyrants of this world, in their blindness, often plant the
seeds of their own destruction. Haman's superstition was
the first step to his ultimate downfall. Rather than seeking
immediate action against the Jews, Haman chose his lucky
day by casting lots. The lot fell on a day 12 months later,
providing ample time for Mordecai and Esther to work to
foil the designs of Haman.

In his approach to the king, Haman showed himself to
be a master of deceit. He said nothing about his own injured
pride and blind hatred but spoke only of the king's "best
interest." He broadened one man's disobedience of a single
decree of the king into the generalization that Jews don't
obey the king's laws. Haman appealed to the king's prejudice by pointing to the Jews' separatism and stirred up the
king's greed by promising great financial returns to the royal
treasury if his program would be carried out. Haman seemed
to be motivated by more than a personal grudge. It appears
he hated the Jews as a people because he resented their religious separatism. He shrewdly refrained from naming the
people he wanted to destroy, lest the king's own knowledge
of the Jews lead him to question Haman's half-truths and

outright lies. It seems incredible that the king would grant Haman's request without more thorough investigation. But Xerxes' action was in keeping with his impetuous character.

Many questions have been raised about the money that Haman promised to the king. Ten thousand talents was a huge amount of money. Some sources claim that it was more than half the annual income of the Persian empire. Such a sum would seem to have been beyond the means of Haman. According to the historian Herodotus, however, this sum was in the same range as the sums that some sub-rulers in Xerxes' empire were capable of raising for the Greek war. It may well be that Haman planned to raise or regain the sum by seizing Jewish property at the time of the massacre. There is some uncertainty about the translation of the king's statement, "Keep the money." Literally it says, "The silver is yours." Some commentators have interpreted this as an ironic remark made by Xerxes when he accepted the money from Haman. It could then be paraphrased: "Well, it's your money. If you want to spend it that way, I'll be glad to take it." Some remarks that appear later in the text imply that the king was going to receive money from Haman, so this interpretation of the text seems preferable to that of the NIV.

Once the deal was struck, the edicts were drawn up and sent throughout the empire. This action agrees well with what we know of the administration and the famous courier system of the Persian Empire. Critics have claimed that the plans to carry out such a large-scale massacre in a single day are unbelievable, but history has recorded other massacres on this scale. In 88 B.C., Mithradates, king of Pontus, massacred 80,000 Romans in one day. He followed this up with a massacre of 20,000 Romans on the small island of Delos. It is shocking that Haman and Xerxes could condemn thousands of men, women, and children to death and then coldly head for a drinking party. But this too is like the conduct of other tyrants in similar circumstances. Perhaps it also reflects an element of truth in Herodotus' claim that after the Persians had made a sober decision, they liked to reconsider it under the influence of alcohol. Be that as it may, the cold-blooded actions of these two tyrants set the stage for the crucial battle to begin.

Meanwhile, the people of Susa were "bewildered." Apparently the decree struck them as strange and arbitrary.

Mordecai's response

4 When Mordecai learned of all that had been done, he tore his clothes, put on sackcloth and ashes, and went out into the city, wailing loudly and bitterly. ²But he went only as far as the king's gate, because no one clothed in sackcloth was allowed to enter it. ³In every province to which the edict and order of the king came, there was great mourning among the Jews, with fasting, weeping and wailing. Many lay in sackcloth and ashes.

⁴When Esther's maids and eunuchs came and told her about Mordecai, she was in great distress. She sent clothes for him to put on instead of his sackcloth, but he would not accept them. ⁵Then Esther summoned Hathach, one of the king's eunuchs assigned to attend her, and ordered him to find out what was troubling Mordecai and why.

⁶So Hathach went out to Mordecai in the open square of the city in front of the king's gate. ⁷Mordecai told him everything that had happened to him, including the exact amount of money Haman had promised to pay into the royal treasury for the destruction of the Jews. ⁸He also gave him a copy of the text of the edict for their annihilation, which had been published in Susa, to show to Esther and explain it to her, and he told him to urge her to go into the king's presence to beg for mercy and plead with him for her people.

⁹Hathach went back and reported to Esther what Mordecai had said. ¹⁰Then she instructed him to say to Mordecai, ¹¹"All the king's officials and the people of the royal provinces know that for any man or woman who approaches the king in the inner court without being summoned the king has but one law: that he be put

to death. The only exception to this is for the king to extend the gold scepter to him and spare his life. But thirty days have passed since I was called to go to the king."

¹²When Esther's words were reported to Mordecai, ¹³he sent back this answer: "Do not think that because you are in the king's house you alone of all the Jews will escape. ¹⁴For if you remain silent at this time, relief and deliverance for the Jews will arise from another place, but you and your father's family will perish. And who knows but that you have come to royal position for such a time as this?"

¹⁵Then Esther sent this reply to Mordecai: ¹⁶"Go, gather together all the Jews who are in Susa, and fast for me. Do not eat or drink for three days, night or day. I and my maids will fast as you do. When this is done, I will go to the king, even though it is against the law. And if I perish, I perish."

¹⁷So Mordecai went away and carried out all of Esther's instructions.

The Jews were shocked when they heard of Haman's plot to destroy them. Mordecai joined in their mourning and displayed the traditional signs of mourning—torn clothes, rough sackcloth garments, and ashes on his face. We do not know whether this indicated a deep religious faith on the part of Mordecai or his actions were only traditional customs of mourning that had lost their spiritual significance for many of the exiles. Elsewhere in the Old Testament, these customs were outward signs of inner repentance and the turning to God for deliverance. For example, Daniel describes how he prayed to the Lord: "I turned to the Lord God and pleaded with him in prayer and petition, in fasting, and in sackcloth and ashes" (Daniel 9:3). But, as is so often the case in the book of Esther, we receive a bare statement of a person's actions without any analysis of his motives.

In the seclusion of the harem, Esther was oblivious to the plot against the Jews until she heard about her step-father's mourning and inquired about its cause. Mordecai warned her of the seriousness of the plot by informing her of the great financial gain that would come to King Xerxes if the plot were carried out. Not only Haman's hatred but also Xerxes' greed had to be overcome if the Jews were to be saved.

Esther tried to excuse herself from helping the Jews by claiming that it would be too dangerous for her to go to King Xerxes without being invited. We have no other knowledge about this Persian custom, except from the Jewish historian Josephus, who wrote much later than the time of Esther. It seems that ancient kings lived under the constant threat of assassination. No one dared to approach the king without an invitation.

The fact that Esther had not been in Xerxes' presence for a month indicates that they did not have a close husband-wife relationship. Given Xerxes' unstable character, Esther may have felt she had fallen from his favor.

Mordecai challenged Esther's reluctance with a mixture of threatening and encouraging words. Esther should not imagine she could escape the decreed fate of all Jews just because she lived in the royal palace. The terms of the decree did not exempt her. If she were too indifferent or fearful to help her people, she should at least take action for her own sake. Mordecai also encouraged her by pointing out that God had always provided deliverance for his people from their oppressors. If Esther failed to use the position to which God had raised her, God would provide another deliverer to make up for her negligence: "If you remain silent at this time, relief and deliverance for the Jews will arise from another place."

Here, as everywhere in the book of Esther, the role of God is present only by implication, not by direct statement. Mordecai merely said, "Who knows but that you have come to royal position for such a time as this?" These are the key words of the book of Esther. Until this time Esther and Mordecai probably did not realize why Esther had become queen of Persia. Perhaps they had even sought the position for her from selfish motives. But now it was clear to Mordecai that God had been working behind the scenes. The Lord was directing the affairs of Persia, so that one of his people would be in a position to help Israel in time of peril. Even at this moment, the Lord was not dependent on Esther. All creation is under his control. If Esther failed to use her position to help her people, God would provide another deliverer. His will would be done, with Esther or without her.

Esther responded to the admonition of Mordecai. The closing verses of this section are the closest thing to an expression of faith that can be found in the book of Esther. Esther's request that all the people join in her fast implies that they should also pray for her, since fasting was regularly a preparation for prayer. On this basis Esther was now determined to go to the king. The words "If I perish, I perish" could be fearless courage or mere resignation. In either case she had made her decision. The showdown was inevitable.

The key principles taught in this section apply also to us. God may provide us with positions, possessions, or talents that enable us to serve the cause of the gospel. We should not let opportunities pass us by. We dare not squander our chances to be of service because we are too fearful to risk our positions or even our lives for the sake of Christ and his gospel. If we are fearful and unfaithful, God will take the opportunities away from us and give them to someone else who will use them for God's glory. If we don't cling to the truths of God's Word, the Lord will raise up someone else who will. If we neglect the task of worldwide missions, the Lord will pass his Word on to other people, who will be eager to share it with others.

God's kingdom will come, either with us or without us. God's will shall be done, either with us or without us. But each time we pray the Lord's Prayer, we are praying that his will may be done by us and that his kingdom will come, in part, through our efforts. God gives us opportunities to be his coworkers in the work of the gospel. Let us pray that we never let our golden chances slip by. If we do, we ourselves will be the losers.

PART TWO

The Delivery of the Jews
(5:1–10:3)

Esther's plan

Esther prepares a banquet

5 On the third day Esther put on her royal robes and stood in the inner court of the palace, in front of the king's hall. The king was sitting on his royal throne in the hall, facing the entrance. ²When he saw Queen Esther standing in the court, he was pleased with her and held out to her the gold scepter that was in his hand. So Esther approached and touched the tip of the scepter.

³Then the king asked, "What is it, Queen Esther? What is your request? Even up to half the kingdom, it will be given you."

⁴"If it pleases the king," replied Esther, "let the king, together with Haman, come today to a banquet I have prepared for him."

⁵"Bring Haman at once," the king said, "so that we may do what Esther asks."

So the king and Haman went to the banquet Esther had prepared. ⁶As they were drinking wine, the king again asked Esther, "Now what is your petition? It will be given you. And what is your request? Even up to half the kingdom, it will be granted."

⁷Esther replied, "My petition and my request is this: ⁸If the king regards me with favor and if it pleases the king to grant my petition and fulfill my request, let the king and Haman come tomorrow to the banquet I will prepare for them. Then I will answer the king's question."

After she had prepared herself spiritually with fasting and prayer, Esther prepared herself physically for her encounter with the king. She put on her beautiful royal robes. We do not have much information about the arrangement of the king's private living quarters or his state reception rooms, but it appears that Esther approached the king in some sort of state reception area that was normally off-limits to her. He was pleased with her, most likely because of her beauty, and extravagantly offered her virtually anything she wanted. Xerxes' promise reminds us of one made by King Herod Antipas to a dancing girl. Herod also promised, "Whatever you ask I will give you, up to half my kingdom" (Mark 6:23). What that girl asked for—and got—was the head of John the Baptist on a platter!

The historian Herodotus records another occasion on which Xerxes made a rash promise to a young woman whom he desired. Herodotus characterizes Xerxes as a rash, impetuous man with a roving eye, who was easily swayed by feminine beauty. The Lord used even the flaws of Xerxes' character to set up the situation in which God would provide deliverance for his people.

Esther's request was simple—that the king and Haman join her for a banquet. Her request was readily granted, but for some reason she failed to act decisively. When the king asked what she wanted, Esther stalled by asking that the king and Haman return for another banquet. She may have had a good reason for thinking that another occasion would offer a better chance of success, or she may simply have lost her nerve. When we look ahead in the story, we realize that regardless of what Esther's motive may have been, the delay was a result of God's providence. This delay was necessary so that the events recorded in the next two sections of our text could take place and prepare the way for Haman's downfall.

Haman continues to plot

⁹Haman went out that day happy and in high spirits. But when he saw Mordecai at the king's gate and observed that he neither

rose nor showed fear in his presence, he was filled with rage against Mordecai. ¹⁰Nevertheless, Haman restrained himself and went home.

Calling together his friends and Zeresh, his wife, ¹¹Haman boasted to them about his vast wealth, his many sons, and all the ways the king had honored him and how he had elevated him above the other nobles and officials. ¹²"And that's not all," Haman added, "I'm the only person Queen Esther invited to accompany the king to the banquet she gave. And she has invited me along with the king tomorrow. ¹³But all this gives me no satisfaction as long as I see that Jew Mordecai sitting at the king's gate."

¹⁴His wife Zeresh and all his friends said to him, "Have a gallows built, seventy-five feet high, and ask the king in the morning to have Mordecai hanged on it. Then go with the king to the dinner and be happy." This suggestion delighted Haman, and he had the gallows built.

"Pride goes before destruction, a haughty spirit before a fall" (Proverbs 16:18). These words of wisdom warn us not to copy the folly of Haman. God brings down the proud. He humbles those who glorify themselves for what they have and who are blind to the goodness of the Creator, who gives everything they have. In this section we also see how the sins of jealousy and holding a grudge can blot out a person's enjoyment of life. Outwardly Haman had everything going for him. He had riches, prestige, and power. He had the special honor of a private banquet with the king and queen. But because of the rage within him, he wasn't able to enjoy what he had. Resentment and an unforgiving spirit were like acid inside Haman; they ate away at any happiness he might have found in his exalted position. Only revenge could give him the satisfaction he desired.

Haman found his joy not in the many good things that he had, but in the plotting of the destruction of the hated Jew Mordecai. There was no sensible reason for a 75-foot gallows (literally, "50 cubits"), so we can offer no explana-

The chronicles are read to the king

tion for it other than the senselessness of Haman's rage. The height of the gallows is not mentioned in the narrative part of the text but only in the words of the speakers. Consequently, some commentators have suggested that the 75 feet is not to be taken literally but is the kind of language we use when we say, "That box weighs a ton," or "I've told you a million times." Nevertheless, the extreme size seems to fit Haman's tremendous ego.

As he prepared the gallows, Haman blindly plowed ahead, oblivious to the fact that he was preparing the instrument of his own destruction.

The rise of Mordecai and downfall of Haman

Mordecai is honored

6 That night the king could not sleep; so he ordered the book of the chronicles, the record of his reign, to be brought in and read to him. ²It was found recorded there that Mordecai had exposed Bigthana and Teresh, two of the king's officers who guarded the doorway, who had conspired to assassinate King Xerxes.

³"What honor and recognition has Mordecai received for this?" the king asked.

"Nothing has been done for him," his attendants answered.

⁴The king said, "Who is in the court?" Now Haman had just entered the outer court of the palace to speak to the king about hanging Mordecai on the gallows he had erected for him.

⁵His attendants answered, "Haman is standing in the court."

"Bring him in," the king ordered.

⁶When Haman entered, the king asked him, "What should be done for the man the king delights to honor?"

Now Haman thought to himself, "Who is there that the king would rather honor than me?" ⁷So he answered the king, "For the man the king delights to honor, ⁸have them bring a royal robe the king has worn and a horse the king has ridden, one with a royal crest placed on its head. ⁹Then let the robe and horse be entrusted to one of the king's most noble princes. Let them robe the man the king delights to honor, and lead him on the horse through the city streets, proclaiming before him, 'This is what is done for the man the king delights to honor!'"

¹⁰"Go at once," the king commanded Haman. "Get the robe and the horse and do just as you have suggested for Mordecai the Jew, who sits at the king's gate. Do not neglect anything you have recommended."

¹¹So Haman got the robe and the horse. He robed Mordecai, and led him on horseback through the city streets, proclaiming before him, "This is what is done for the man the king delights to honor!"

¹²Afterward Mordecai returned to the king's gate. But Haman rushed home, with his head covered in grief, ¹³and told Zeresh his wife and all his friends everything that had happened to him.

His advisers and his wife Zeresh said to him, "Since Mordecai, before whom your downfall has started, is of Jewish origin, you cannot stand against him—you will surely come to ruin!" ¹⁴While they were still talking with him, the king's eunuchs arrived and hurried Haman away to the banquet Esther had prepared.

Here, as is so often the case, the author of Esther does not overwhelm us with commentary and explanation. The irony and appropriateness of the events in the text speak for themselves. The skeptic might call these events luck. We see them as a magnificent display of the providence of God.

On the very night when the future of Israel hung in the balance, the king could not sleep and requested reading material. He "just happened" to open the book to the very spot that reminded him that he owed Mordecai a reward. And Haman "just happened" to be entering the court at that very moment.

The king concealed the identity of the Jew whom he desired to reward, just as Haman had concealed the identity of the Jews whom he desired to destroy. Haman

Mordecai is honored

was so vain that he could not imagine anyone else the king could possibly want to reward more than him. He heaped up the honors, thinking that they would all fall on him.

The king's words "for Mordecai the Jew" are recorded rather matter-of-factly. But we can well imagine how they must have hit Haman like a ton of bricks. Imagine the expression on his face! So the ultimate irony took place when Haman had to honor the Jew whom he wished to destroy.

This reversal of fortunes was so shocking that Haman's wife and advisors—and no doubt Haman himself—were convinced that he was doomed. Suddenly, before he could gather his thoughts, he was swept off to the queen's banquet. Certainly the hope must have flashed through his mind, "I can still be saved since I enjoy the special favor of the queen."

The downfall of Haman

7 **So the king and Haman went to dine with Queen Esther, ²and as they were drinking wine on that second day, the king again asked, "Queen Esther, what is your petition? It will be given you. What is your request? Even up to half the kingdom, it will be granted."**

³ᵀThen Queen Esther answered, "If I have found favor with you, O king, and if it pleases your majesty, grant me my life—this is my petition. And spare my people—this is my request. ⁴For I and my people have been sold for destruction and slaughter and annihilation. If we had merely been sold as male and female slaves, I would have kept quiet, because no such distress would justify disturbing the king."

⁵King Xerxes asked Queen Esther, "Who is he? Where is the man who has dared to do such a thing?"

⁶Esther said, "The adversary and enemy is this vile Haman."

Then Haman was terrified before the king and queen. ⁷The king got up in a rage, left his wine and went out into the palace garden. But Haman, realizing that the king had already decided his fate, stayed behind to beg Queen Esther for his life.

⁸Just as the king returned from the palace garden to the banquet hall, Haman was falling on the couch where Esther was reclining.

The king exclaimed, "Will he even molest the queen while she is with me in the house?"

As soon as the word left the king's mouth, they covered Haman's face. ⁹Then Harbona, one of the eunuchs attending the king, said, "A gallows seventy-five feet high stands by Haman's house. He had it made for Mordecai, who spoke up to help the king."

The king said, "Hang him on it!" ¹⁰So they hanged Haman on the gallows he had prepared for Mordecai. Then the king's fury subsided.

As the banquet began, Esther probably did not yet know about the exaltation of Mordecai. She may still have dreaded the great power of Haman, but she was emboldened when the king repeated his lavish promise. Using the same cleverness shown by Haman, Esther did not tip her hand by naming her people. She based her appeal on the king's feelings for her. Even at this point the king apparently did not realize that she was talking about the Jews, whose condemnation Haman had achieved.

It may strike us as strange that Esther said it would not even have been worth it to bother the king if the Jews were merely being sold into slavery. Esther may simply have been using the language of extreme deference to royalty here; but a different translation of this difficult verse is also possible. According to the alternate translation offered in the NIV footnote, Esther said that she would not have complained just for the sake of the Jews, but that her first concern was for the king. The loss of service the king would suffer if the Jews were destroyed would be greater than the gain of money that Haman had promised him. If we follow this understanding, then Esther presented her case as if her main concern were to safeguard the best interests of the king. Regardless of which interpretation of the verse is followed, Esther's approach to the king was a masterpiece of diplomacy.

Once again the whole situation is most ironic. We have seen Xerxes, the great world ruler, first condemn and then reprieve the Jews without ever really realizing what was going on either time!

When the king was moved by Esther's plea, Esther dramatically exposed "vile" Haman, who was dumbstruck by the sudden turn of events. Haman knew the hot temper of the king all too well and realized that his only hope was to have Esther intercede for him. If we did not know better, we would think it was just terribly "bad luck" that Haman fell on the queen at the very moment in which the king returned to the banquet hall. But by now we recognize the ruling hand of God, who directs all things so they turn out for the good of his people.

The fatal fall sealed Haman's doom. Covering his face apparently was a symbol of his condemnation to death, but we know little about Persian customs in this regard. When Haman was hanged on his own gallows, it was an example of the truth of the proverbs, "If a man digs a pit, he will fall into it; if a man rolls a stone, it will roll back on him" (Proverbs 26:27).

The persecutor was cast down as quickly as he had risen, but God's people were not yet free from danger.

The triumph of the Jews

The king's edict in behalf of the Jews

8 That same day King Xerxes gave Queen Esther the estate of Haman, the enemy of the Jews. And Mordecai came into the presence of the king, for Esther had told how he was related to her. ²The king took off his signet ring, which he had reclaimed from Haman, and presented it to Mordecai. And Esther appointed him over Haman's estate.

³Esther again pleaded with the king, falling at his feet and weeping. She begged him to put an end to the evil plan of Haman the Agagite, which he had devised against the Jews. ⁴Then the king extended the gold scepter to Esther and she arose and stood before him.

⁵"If it pleases the king," she said, "and if he regards me with favor and thinks it the right thing to do, and if he is pleased with me, let an order be written overruling the dispatches that Haman son of Hammedatha, the Agagite, devised and wrote to destroy the Jews in all the king's provinces. ⁶For how can I bear to see disaster fall on my people? How can I bear to see the destruction of my family?"

⁷King Xerxes replied to Queen Esther and to Mordecai the Jew, "Because Haman attacked the Jews, I have given his estate to Esther, and they have hanged him on the gallows. ⁸Now write another decree in the king's name in behalf of the Jews as seems best to you, and seal it with the king's signet ring—for no document written in the king's name and sealed with his ring can be revoked."

⁹At once the royal secretaries were summoned—on the twenty-third day of the third month, the month of Sivan. They wrote out all Mordecai's orders to the Jews, and to the satraps, governors and nobles of the 127 provinces stretching from India to Cush. These orders were written in the script of each province and the language of each people and also to the Jews in their own script and language. ¹⁰Mordecai wrote in the name of King Xerxes, sealed the dispatches with the king's signet ring, and sent them by mounted couriers, who rode fast horses especially bred for the king.

¹¹The king's edict granted the Jews in every city the right to assemble and protect themselves; to destroy, kill and annihilate any armed force of any nationality or province that might attack them and their women and children; and to plunder the property of their

enemies. ¹²The day appointed for the Jews to do this in all the provinces of King Xerxes was the thirteenth day of the twelfth month, the month of Adar. ¹³A copy of the text of the edict was to be issued as law in every province and made known to the people of every nationality so that the Jews would be ready on that day to avenge themselves on their enemies.

¹⁴The couriers, riding the royal horses, raced out, spurred on by the king's command. And the edict was also issued in the citadel of Susa.

¹⁵Mordecai left the king's presence wearing royal garments of blue and white, a large crown of gold and a purple robe of fine linen. And the city of Susa held a joyous celebration. ¹⁶For the Jews it was a time of happiness and joy, gladness and honor. ¹⁷In every province and in every city, wherever the edict of the king went, there was joy and gladness among the Jews, with feasting and celebrating. And many people of other nationalities became Jews because fear of the Jews had seized them.

Although Haman had been eliminated, the threat to the Jews remained, because the royal decree authorizing their slaughter had already been published. Since the time for the execution of the decree was still ten months away, we might think that the easiest solution would be for the king to revoke the decree. But according to the Persian regulation reported earlier in the book of Esther (1:19), Persian royal decrees could not be revoked. The only way to get around the decree was to issue a second decree that would have the practical effect of rendering the first decree harmless. With the guidance of Mordecai, King Xerxes issued such a decree.

The Jews now had ten months to strengthen themselves and prepare their defenses. It is shocking to us that the decree authorized the killing of women and children. But this decree was merely following the basic principle of Near Eastern justice, which is also recognized in the Mosaic Law—"[an] eye for [an] eye" (Deuteronomy 19:21).

This decree authorized the Jews to use the exact measures that Haman's decree, recorded in chapter 4, had granted to their enemies. Both sides in the conflict were now put on equal terms.

Esther had gained this decree by again taking advantage of the king's favor for her. Mordecai then put the decree into effect, as he took over Haman's position of influence and his wealth as well. The decree was rapidly spread throughout the vast empire by the excellent Persian courier system. The Jews throughout the empire celebrated the dramatic turn of events and Mordecai's rise to prominence. Although the final outcome of the decree was still ten months away, the Jews' victory seemed assured. Many people allied themselves with the Jews in order to share their triumph.

The edict carried out

9 **On the thirteenth day of the twelfth month, the month of Adar, the edict commanded by the king was to be carried out. On this day the enemies of the Jews had hoped to overpower them, but now the tables were turned and the Jews got the upper hand over those who hated them. ²The Jews assembled in their cities in all the provinces of King Xerxes to attack those seeking their destruction. No one could stand against them, because the people of all the other nationalities were afraid of them. ³And all the nobles of the provinces, the satraps, the governors and the king's administrators helped the Jews, because fear of Mordecai had seized them. ⁴Mordecai was prominent in the palace; his reputation spread throughout the provinces, and he became more and more powerful.**

⁵The Jews struck down all their enemies with the sword, killing and destroying them, and they did what they pleased to those who hated them. ⁶In the citadel of Susa, the Jews killed and destroyed five hundred men. ⁷They also killed Parshandatha, Dalphon, Aspatha, ⁸Poratha, Adalia, Aridatha, ⁹Parmashta, Arisai, Ardai and

Vaizatha, ¹⁰the ten sons of Haman son of Hammedatha, the enemy of the Jews. But they did not lay their hands on the plunder.

¹¹The number of those slain in the citadel of Susa was reported to the king that same day. ¹²The king said to Queen Esther, "The Jews have killed and destroyed five hundred men and the ten sons of Haman in the citadel of Susa. What have they done in the rest of the king's provinces? Now what is your petition? It will be given you. What is your request? It will also be granted."

¹³"If it pleases the king," Esther answered, "give the Jews in Susa permission to carry out this day's edict tomorrow also, and let Haman's ten sons be hanged on gallows."

¹⁴So the king commanded that this be done. An edict was issued in Susa, and they hanged the ten sons of Haman. ¹⁵The Jews in Susa came together on the fourteenth day of the month of Adar, and they put to death in Susa three hundred men, but they did not lay their hands on the plunder.

¹⁶Meanwhile, the remainder of the Jews who were in the king's provinces also assembled to protect themselves and get relief from their enemies. They killed seventy-five thousand of them but did not lay their hands on the plunder. ¹⁷This happened on the thirteenth day of the month of Adar, and on the fourteenth they rested and made it a day of feasting and joy.

When the crucial day arrived, the Jews eliminated their enemies. In the capital city alone, they killed eight hundred men in two days. This included the ten sons of Haman, who were executed one day and hung on gallows (the word can also mean "poles") the next. The empire-wide total of 75,000 seems incredibly large, but it is not larger than the toll of other similar uprisings or reprisals recorded in history. Shocking as it is, there is nothing inherently improbable about it. It is also true to human nature that non-Jewish officials were quick to jump to the Jews' assistance when they thought that such an action would gain them favor with the powerful Mordecai. Many people, including many Jewish writers, are distressed and question the morality of such a slaughter. Especially disturbing is Esther's request for another day to attack the enemies. As usual, the book of Esther offers no evaluation of the motives of the various participants. We need not assume that all who took part in the destruction of the enemies acted out of pure motives of self-defense. There may have been a vengeful spirit on the part of some of the Jews. On the other hand, the account demonstrates that the Jews tried to protect themselves from charges of malice and selfishness. They didn't take any plunder from the victims, in order to protect themselves from charges of killing others simply to enrich themselves. There is no indication that they took advantage of the king's permission to kill women and children. The text tries to emphasize that the Jewish attack on their enemies was a defensive attack: "to protect themselves and get relief from their enemies." If the Jews did not strike their enemies at this time, the enemies might regain the king's favor and recover their power to attack the Jews on another occasion. The Jews felt compelled to fight the battle to its conclusion while they had the upper hand.

It's clear from all this that Haman's edict had appealed to a widespread hatred for the Jews. It seems that Haman and many others had been looking for an opportunity to persecute the Jews. Naturally the Jews lived in dread of another such decree.

Nevertheless, the real purpose of the scriptural account is not to excuse or defend the action of the Jews. Rather, it is to show how God acted in history to preserve his chosen people, so that the promise of the Messiah could be fulfilled. God used the actions and motives of everyone involved— whether they were good or bad—toward the ultimate outcome of the preservation of his people. Whether the motives of Esther and Mordecai were pure, mixed, or selfish, the main point of the story remains the same: God controls history to preserve his people and fulfill his promises.

The celebration of Purim

[18]The Jews in Susa, however, had assembled on the thirteenth and fourteenth, and then on the fifteenth they rested and made it a day of feasting and joy.

[19]That is why rural Jews—those living in villages—observe the fourteenth of the month of Adar as a day of joy and feasting, a day for giving presents to each other.

[20]Mordecai recorded these events, and he sent letters to all the Jews throughout the provinces of King Xerxes, near and far, [21]to have them celebrate annually the fourteenth and fifteenth days of the month of Adar [22]as the time when the Jews got relief from their enemies, and as the month when their sorrow was turned into joy and their mourning into a day of celebration. He wrote them to observe the days as days of feasting and joy and giving presents of food to one another and gifts to the poor.

[23]So the Jews agreed to continue the celebration they had begun, doing what Mordecai had written to them. [24]For Haman son of Hammedatha, the Agagite, the enemy of all the Jews, had plotted against the Jews to destroy them and had cast the *pur* (that is, the lot) for their ruin and destruction. [25]But when the plot came to the king's attention, he issued written orders that the evil scheme Haman had devised against the Jews should come back onto his own head, and that he and his sons should be hanged on the gallows. [26](Therefore these days were called Purim, from the word *pur*.) Because of everything written in this letter and because of what they had seen and what had happened to them, [27]the Jews took it upon themselves to establish the custom that they and their descendants and all who join them should without fail observe these two days every year, in the way prescribed and at the time appointed. [28]These days should be remembered and observed in every generation by every family, and in every province and in every city. And these days of Purim should never cease to be celebrated by the

Jews, nor should the memory of them die out among their descendants.

²⁹So Queen Esther, daughter of Abihail, along with Mordecai the Jew, wrote with full authority to confirm this second letter concerning Purim. ³⁰And Mordecai sent letters to all the Jews in the 127 provinces of the kingdom of Xerxes—words of good will and assurance—³¹to establish these days of Purim at their designated times, as Mordecai the Jew and Queen Esther had decreed for them, and as they had established for themselves and their descendants in regard to their times of fasting and lamentation. ³²Esther's decree confirmed these regulations about Purim, and it was written down in the records.

This section shows how Purim became a major holiday in the Jewish calendar and received recognition, along with Passover, Pentecost (also called Weeks, or Harvest), and Tabernacles, the three major festivals commanded by God through Moses (Leviticus 23:5-8; Numbers 28:26; Leviticus 23:34-44). Esther and Mordecai used their positions of influence in the government to send directives to the Jews throughout the empire to celebrate their deliverance with a new holiday, called Purim. This name came from the word *pur*, the word for the lots Haman had cast. This was an appropriate name for the holiday since the casting of lots by Haman had postponed the destruction of the Jews by a year and allowed time for Haman's downfall and the undoing of the decree. Already at the first stage of Haman's plot, God had intervened in order to thwart him. Heathen would call the outcome of the lots fate, and most modern people would call it luck, but we recognize it as the hand of God.

We do not know how readily religious Jews accepted a holiday ordered by secular leaders who were not priests or prophets of God. But Purim became established as a Jewish holiday and is still celebrated. It is not mentioned in the

New Testament but is mentioned in the Apocrypha and by Josephus. Shortly after the time of Christ, a whole section of the worship regulations recorded in the Jewish traditions, the Mishnah, was devoted to this holiday.

Purim usually occurs during our month of February. Its celebration is somewhat like a combination of Halloween and New Year's Eve. Children wear costumes and paint their faces. There is a great deal of merrymaking. A very important aspect of the holiday is the public reading of the book of Esther. This reading is interrupted with noisemakers and the singing of festive songs at every mention of Haman's name. Gifts of food to friends and to the poor are another part of the holiday. One unique food of the festival is a cookie called Haman's ears. The whole tone of the holiday is that of a victory celebration, like V-E (Victory in Europe) Day or V-J (Victory over Japan) Day or Armistice Day in modern times.

Recognizing and remembering God's intervention in history to save his people is more important than celebrating the triumph of a people over its enemies. The real purpose of this story is not to boost the national pride of the Israelites but to proclaim the glory of the faithful God who sustained them. God gives relief to his persecuted people and trouble to those who trouble them. From time to time in history, he intervenes to deliver his people. On judgment day he will fully vindicate his persecuted remnant. The book of Esther is an outstanding example of such intervention, recalling the words of David: "He who avenges blood remembers; he does not ignore the cry of the afflicted" (Psalm 9:12).

The greatness of Mordecai

10 King Xerxes imposed tribute throughout the empire, to its distant shores. ²And all his acts of power and might,

together with a full account of the greatness of Mordecai to which the king had raised him, are they not written in the book of the annals of the kings of Media and Persia? ³Mordecai the Jew was second in rank to King Xerxes, preeminent among the Jews, and held in high esteem by his many fellow Jews, because he worked for the good of his people and spoke up for the welfare of all the Jews.

This final, brief chapter is a postscript to the book of Esther. It describes the greatness of Xerxes and Mordecai after the overthrow of Haman. The main purpose of this addition is to assure the readers of the historical accuracy of the account by referring them to the Persian records in which they can find verification of the story and more information about Mordecai. Whether verified by outside history or not, we can be confident that all Bible history is true. It is part of God's inerrant Word.

Xerxes is mentioned to show that he did not suffer loss by befriending the Jews and spurning Haman's money. On the contrary, he remained as great as ever, collecting tribute throughout his vast empire. Moreover, it would have been offensive for the writer of Esther, who was probably affiliated with the Persian court, to praise Mordecai without at least a nod of recognition to the Persian monarch.

This postscript also gives Mordecai the recognition and honor he deserved for his faithful service to God's people. We should also remember with love and respect those who have served God's people faithfully, especially those who have served in the preaching and teaching ministries. When we are thankful for these heroes of the faith, we are also thankful for the God who gave them.

Conclusion to Ezra, Nehemiah, Esther

The three books we have just studied show us some of the best examples of God's loving care for his people. God's preservation of his people recorded in these three books was not as spectacular as the deliverance from Pharaoh recorded in Exodus. Yet it was just as important and just as much of a testimony to God's power. Because of the mighty signs that Moses performed, he was a more spectacular leader than Zerubbabel, Jeshua, Ezra, Nehemiah, Esther, or Mordecai. But each of these leaders played a role in God's plan for preserving his people until the Savior would come. God worked quietly through these people. He also worked powerfully so that the stage was set for Christ's appearance.

These three books bring Old Testament history to an end. Four hundred years would still pass before the Savior's birth, but the story of how God preserved his promise of the Messiah from Eden to Bethlehem had been told. The forces of Satan had been unsuccessful in their countless attempts to destroy the seed of the woman and prevent the coming of the Savior. During the four hundred-year span between Nehemiah and John the Baptist, God continued to keep the Jews from dangerous enemies.

When the story of God's love resumes with Jesus' birth, the goal of all Old Testament history has been reached. The Seed of the woman (Genesis 3:15) arrives to crush the serpent's head. The salvation that the Old Testament believers longed to see finally comes when God's Son appears on earth to do away with sin.

With this glorious event the real purpose of the stories of Ezra, Nehemiah, and Esther is fulfilled.

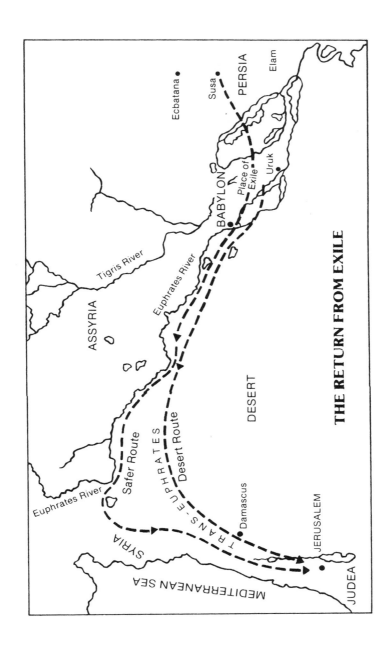

THE RETURN FROM EXILE

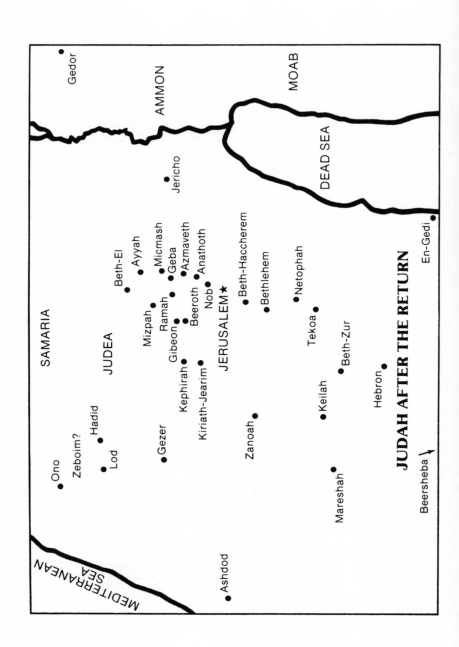

JUDAH AFTER THE RETURN

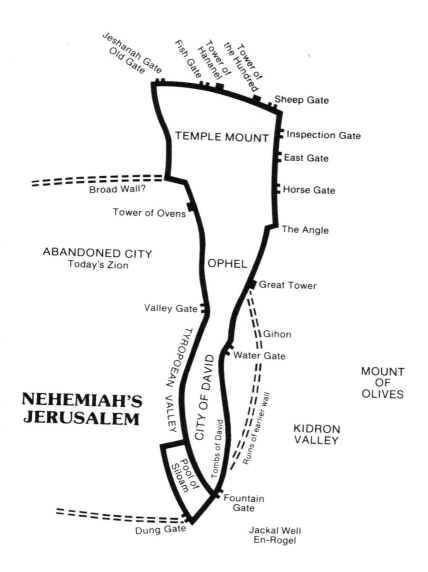

NEHEMIAH'S JERUSALEM

Jeshanah Gate
Old Gate

Fish Gate

Tower of Hananel

Tower of the Hundred

Sheep Gate

TEMPLE MOUNT

Inspection Gate

East Gate

Broad Wall?

Horse Gate

Tower of Ovens

The Angle

ABANDONED CITY
Today's Zion

OPHEL

Great Tower

Valley Gate

Gihon

TYROPOEAN VALLEY

Water Gate

CITY OF DAVID

MOUNT OF OLIVES

Tombs of David

Ruins of earlier wall

KIDRON VALLEY

Pool of Siloam

Fountain Gate

Dung Gate

Jackal Well
En-Rogel

201